The Path of Grace

The Path of Grace

by Shyamdas
Edited by Vallabhdas

Published by:
Pratham Peeth Publications
2010

2nd Edition

Printed by:
Shri Harinam Press, Vrindaban / harinampress@gmail.com

ALSO BY SHYAMDAS

Inner Goddess
In Praise of Vallabh
Eighty-Four Vaishnavas
252 Vaishnavas, Parts 1 – 3
Eighty-Four Seats: Chaurasi Baithak
The Teachings of Shri Vallabhacharya
Ocean of Jewels: The Prameyaratnarnava of Lallu Bhatta
Ocean of Grace: The Teachings of H.H. Goswami Prathameshji
Krishna's Inner Circle: The Ashta Chaap Poets
Shri Harirayaji's 41 Shiksha Patra
The Amazing Story of Sri Nathji
Venu Gita: The Song of the Flute
Loving Wisdom

These and other titles are available in the United States, through
Sacred Woods
www.sacredwoods.net
email: sacred108@aol.com
phone: 1-800-701-1008
and
www.shyamdas.com

In India, from:
www.sacredwoods.net
Deepu Pandit: sacredwoods@rediffmail.com
Girdhar Nivaas, Gokul. Dist. Mathura, U.P.
phone: 0566-127-2256

or

Rasbihari Lal and Sons, Loi Bazaar, Vrindavan
brijwasi2001@hotmail.com

॥विजयते श्रीमन्मथुरायीशप्रभुः॥

गोस्वामी श्री मिलनकुमारजी

शुद्धाद्वैत प्रथम पीठ

कोटा • जतीपुरा • मुम्बई • कोलकाता

Tel: 91-9323248282 • Mumbai: 91-22-26237987 Kota: 91-744-2386826

email: milangoswami@gmail.com

श्री गिरधर निवास प्लाट नं 7, गांधी ग्राम मार्ग

गृह– विले पर्ले (प.) मुंबई – 4000 49

BLESSINGS

I am delighted to see this book, a valuable resource for English speaking Vaishnavas and scholars who seek to understand the essence of Shri Vallabhacharya's devotional path. This clear and concise text covers many aspects of the Pushti Marg and is a welcome addition to its rich literary tradition. Shyamdasji has done a remarkable service by translating the teachings of the Path of Grace into English. My blessings to Shyamdasji for his devotional service on behalf of Mahaprabhu Shri Vallabhacharya.

— *Goswami Milan Kumar*

INTRODUCTION

Shri Mahaprabhu Vallabhacharya (1479-1531 CE) founded the Path of Grace and gifted the world with exalted teachings. He established the premise that this creation is comprised of blissful Divinity and nothing but Divinity. This pure view inspires us to discover the Lord's joy in ourselves and in the world. Shri Vallabhacharya taught his followers to always experience Shri Krishna everywhere and with every feeling. In his Path of Grace we find an unparalleled group of Acharyas and bhaktas who have together produced oceans of philosophy, art, literature and music, all of which are offered in Shri Krishna's pleasing service – His *seva*.

For grace filled souls, the world is not unreal or something to overcome, but rather, a divine realm wherein the experience of Shri Krishna and His manifold creation can be experienced as a *Lila*, a divine play. Shri Vallabhacharya encourages us to live happily in this world and offer our bodies, wealth, hearts and everything to the Lord of Sweetness. Shri Krishna pays close attention to those who adore Him, and He returns every favor hundred fold. To know and love Him is devotion. To experience His rapture is grace. The Path of Grace inspires us to employ our hearts and minds in His pleasure. It encourages us to use our bodies and every resource in a brilliant and sensitive manner, so that we ultimately become possessed by Divinity. In that blessed state, is there even a need for liberation?

Shri Vallabhacharya gathered the drops of nectar overflowing from Shri Krishna's bliss form and from them created a Path of Grace. The climb out of ignorance is too steep, and so Shri Krishna descends to this world, where He plays according to the aptitude of His individual bhaktas.

The collection of Shri Krishna's nectars, inspired towards graceful nourishment, appeared in totality in the form of Shri Vallabhacharya. The great Acharya coupled non-dual devotional view with endless creative expression, all as an offering to the Lord of sweetness. Shri Vallabhacharya's son, Shri Gusainji, further developed the movements of this path, wherein yogis, artists, Brahmins, Muslims, kings and poets all found a common platform of grace filled Krishna devotion. Let us begin our journey on the Path of Grace with the life of *Shri Acharyaji* – Mahaprabhu Shrimad Vallabhacharya.

1.
SHRI MAHAPRABHUJI
VALLABHACHARYA

HIS APPEARANCE

When Joy and Supreme Bliss incarnated as Shri Krishna's own face, a flow of immeasurable grace descended to enlighten divine souls. He became the Beloved, Shri Vallabh – knower of the inner Veda, son of Lakshman Bhatt, sun to the lotus of devotion. When its petals opened, the devotional practice of bhakti was revealed; those who could imbibe its fragrance became Shri Krishna's beloveds. Shri Vallabhacharya's path is grace filled and its principles profound. Compassion is the seed, and nectar is the reward.

When the need for spiritual adjustment arises in this world – when the paths of *dharma* and devotion are covered with the impurities of this age of strife, an incarnation or saint arrives to make the world an easier place to experience the Lord's remarkable presence. Shri Krishna promises in the Gita, "Whenever anti-dharmic forces prevail, I take birth again and again for the establishment of dharma."

During the times of Shri Vallabhacharya's appearance, North India had been conquered by the Mughals. The Vedic dharmas were in distress. Shri Vallabhacharya explained the situation precisely in his short teaching, *Refuge in Krishna*: "All proper spiritual paths have been destroyed in this age of struggle. The practitioners of dharma have become wicked, and hypocrisy is rampant...."

The Ganga and other holy places have been surrounded by wicked people....True knowledge has been lost, along with the proper use of mantras, fasts and yoga. Inner meanings and the *devas* have all become concealed. Krishna alone is my refuge." [1]

It was time for Shri Krishna's face to appear as Shri Vallabh, the giver of the priceless award, the extremely generous one who would not be understood by those engrossed in purely worldly affairs. The scene was ready and the time ripe for the beloved sun of devotion to arrive for the benefit of the pure-hearted.

Shri Vallabhacharya's forefathers were from Kakarwad, a town on the southern banks of the Krishna River in present day Andhra Pradesh. Their family name was Vellanadu. Shri Vallabh's father, Lakshman Bhatt, was a devout Brahmin who performed Soma sacrifices as his ancestors had done. Shri Yajnanarayan Bhatt, Lakshman Bhatt's great, great grandfather, began the family practice of performing Soma sacrifices. He was charitable to his people. During the course of one Soma sacrifice, a *svarupa*, the very image of Lord Krishna, appeared in the sacrificial fire. At that time, the voice of the Lord spoke to Shri Yajnanarayan Bhatt, "I will appear in your family after one hundred soma sacrifices have been completed."

Yajnanarayan's son, Shri Gangadhara performed twenty-eight additional Soma sacrifices. His son, Shri Ganapati Bhatt continued the tradition and reinforced Vedic teachings during his lifetime. His son, Shri Bal Bhatt completed five sacrifices. He had two sons, Shri Lakshman and Shri Janardan. Shri Lakshman married Illamagaru, the daughter of Shri Susharma, the royal priest of the prominent South Indian Hindu kingdom of Vidyanagar.

Shri Vallabhacharya's father, Lakshman Bhatt, was a Tailanga Brahmin and also lived in Kakarwad. He too was

steeped in Vedic culture and practice. After the birth of a son
-and two daughters, Lakshman Bhatt decided to renounce
the world, but a sage dissuaded him from doing so.
Lakshman Bhatt spent his time in devotion to Gopal Krishna
and undertook pilgrimages to many holy places before
eventually settling in Benares. He was aware of the fact that
the Lord would appear in his family, for he had completed
his family's one hundredth Soma sacrifice, but he wondered
how and when this appearance would take place.

When Muslim disturbance threatened Benares,
Lakshman Bhatt and his family fled towards South India,
where Hindu kingdoms still dominated. Along the way he
halted at Champaranya, near Raipura in Madhya Pradesh.
There his pregnant wife Illamagaru suddenly gave birth, two
months prematurely, to what appeared to be a still-born
baby. The parents sadly placed the infant inside a hollow of
a tree and retreated to a nearby village. That evening, the
Blessed Lord appeared to Illamagaru in a dream and told her,
"I have appeared as your son!"

They immediately returned to the tree and were both
astonished and delighted to find a living, glowing baby,
surrounded by a ring of fire! Shri Vallabh's ecstatic mother
extended her arms into the fire and received her divine child
happily to her breast, unscathed by the flames.

Fire is a significant element throughout Shri
Vallabhacharya's life. He is considered to be the incarnation
of *Agni*, or fire. Fire is also the *devata* (deity) of speech, and
so he is called Vak Pati, the Lord of Speech.

They named the infant 'Vallabh,' which means
'Beloved.' Shri Vallabh's extraordinary birth made Lakshman
Bhatt realize that the prophecy of his forefathers had finally
come to fruition. It was a time for celebration indeed. One
of Vallabhacharya's followers, Harija had the vision of the
Master's appearance and sang,

O mother, Shri Mahaprabhu Vallabh has appeared!
  There are great celebrations in his father's home.
O mother, I sing a sweet song
  of how the blessed people have come to see.
O mother, the Brahmins are reciting the Vedas.
  They are giving beautiful blessings.
O mother, the square is adorned with pearls,
  and bards are singing his praises.
O mother, in every home drums sound.
  Flowers rain from the sky.
O mother, clothes are gifted.
  Men and women are wearing them.
O mother, blessed is Shri Vallabh's mother.
  All of her desires are now fulfilled.
Sing's Harija, "On that day
  there were abundant pleasures."

SHRI VALLABH'S VIEW

When social and political conditions improved, Lakshman Bhatt returned to Benares and began Shri Vallabh's education. He engaged the best tutors to impart knowledge of the Vedic systems to his son in Sanskrit. Shri Vallabh's education commenced at the age of seven with the study of the four Vedas, each taught under a different specialist. By the age of ten he had acquired mastery over not only the six systems of Indian philosophy, but also the philosophical systems of Shri Shankara, Shri Ramanuja, Shri Madhva, Shri Nimbark, as well as Jainism and Buddhism. His erudition and intellect amazed everyone. He was called "The Wisdom Child" and "The Master of Speech."

Shri Vallabh's main interest was reading *Shrimad Bhagavatam*, the sacred text that reveals Shri Krishna's lilas. He was particularly fond of the *Rasa Lila* chapters wherein the Blessed Lord dances with thousands of Gopis, enlightened dairymaids, under Vrindavan's autumn full moon. His father's home was adorned with wall paintings depicting the divine event, and Shri Vallabh often sat before them, oblivious to everything else. He understood the inner essence of the Rasa Lila, Shri Krishna's congregation of nectars.

Shri Vallabh was a genius of dharma astonished everyone with his wisdom. He considered his ultimate gurus to be the Gopis of Vrindavan and concluded that Shri Krishna is the means as well as the reward and appears before those who have pure devotion. From childhood he taught a Path of Grace wherein everything is saturated with devotion and known through love. Shri Vallabh focused on the Gopis of Vrindavan, the gurus of *bhakti* (devotion) and their lovely lilas with Shri Krishna within their homes. He knew that everything can be attained by emulating their bhakti. The story of love is an amazing affair. Shri Vallabh's conclusion was, "Always, with every divine feeling, worship Shri Krishna, the Lord of Gokul."[2]

Shri Vallabh fashioned his teachings to fit into the world, which he taught as being Shri Krishna's perfect creation. He viewed the world as Shri Krishna's playground and urged his followers to offer Krishna things of the highest quality. This inspired oceans of art, music and poetry to emerge in his Path of Grace, and Shri Krishna clearly began to respond to His blessed devotees. Poets, artists, writers, kings, Muslim mystics, pundits and even a few animals gained entrance into the Path of Grace and tasted the nectar of devotion. This path of intense Radha-Krishna worship was embraced by the greatest poets of the times, such as Surdas and Paramananda Das.

Shri Vallabh's manifestation was multi-leveled. To some he simply appeared as the son of Lakshman, to others great pundit, and to some, a guru. His intimate disciples knew Shri Vallabh to be not only the incarnation of both Shri Swamini and Shri Krishna, but Their witness as well. From his unique position, he urged his followers to make Shri Krishna's seva, His loving service, in their daily lives. He taught them to emulate the Gopis' ways of selfless devotion to direct their minds and hearts towards Shri Krishna. He urged his blessed ones to follow Shri Krishna's movements throughout the day. His Path became known as the Pushti Marg, "The Path of Grace."

DIVINE CAUSE

Shri Vallabhacharya's appearance here on earth had a divine cause, linked to the following occurrence. Shri Krishna once desired to dance with Shri Swaminiji. When she showed no interest, Shri Krishna, the Master of all things, made another divine creation and danced there. When Shri Swaminiji saw Him dancing without Her, She went to her Beloved and pulled on His necklace. The necklace broke, and when all the gems scattered onto the earth, the divine couple realized that the fallen jewels were actually divine souls connected to Them.

They immediately felt intense separation from those divine souls, and two columns of fire emanated from Their hearts. Beloved Vallabh manifested where the two fire columns converged. He is a combination of Shri Krishna's love for Shri Swaminiji and Shri Swaminiji's love for Shri Krishna, as well as Their witness. The intensity that issued from Them and created beloved Vallabh made him the divine Fire God, for he was filled with Their intensity. Beloved Vallabh then appeared on the earth to collect the dispersed divine souls and remind them, "Remember, dear soul! You have been separated from Beloved Krishna for thousands of births. You have forgotten the nectar of His union. Do you feel the sweet pangs of His separation?" The search for these divine souls inspired Shri Vallabh to undertake three pilgrimages around the four corners of India.

The Vallabh lineage also originates from the line of Rudra. The word *rudra* means literally "to cry." Shri Vallabhacharya's intense path of love contains the essence of the divine tears that the Gopis shed while they sought their blessed Lord in the bowers of Vrindavan. A bhakta describes the cause of Shri Vallabhacharya's appearance:

"O, Vallabh!
You have appeared to show
the blessed way.
You are a giver of joy,
the very form of Supreme Bliss,
a grace filled treasure....
You have appeared to reveal the loving ways in which
the Gopis worshipped Shri Krishna,
for the benefit of the world."

CHILD WANDERINGS

Even as a child, young Vallabh never wore any sewn cloth or anything on his feet. He wore only a light cotton dhoti and shawl, even when traveling in the high mountain regions of the Himalayas. The eleven year old's lotus feet purified the earth wherever he went. Vallabh knew that the path of devotion needed to be resurrected. The teachings of Shri Shankaracharya had swept through India. Shri Vallabh felt that Shri Shankar's teachings – wherein the world and ultimately even Shri Krishna were considered false, and devotion inferior to knowledge, were misleading the people. Shri Vallabh's mission was to revive the Vedantic truth of the

One joyous Lord who lives in all things, whose creations are free of fault and *maya* (illusion), and who can be known through dedication and selfless devotion.

As his son, Shri Vitthalnathji wrote in *Sarvottama Stotram*, 108 names in praise of Shri Vallabh, "He defeated the theories which state that the world is comprised of illusory maya and dispelled the confusion of all other false teachings."[3] Shri Vallabh saw everything as purely Krishna and only Krishna. He is the purest non-dualist.

Shri Vallabh's divine assignment was manifold. It required the young Master to wander extensively in order to spread the light of devotion according to Vedic wisdom, to clarify the paths of practice, and most importantly, to reunite divine souls with their eternal Lord. He was not interested in mass conversion, for he is "intent upon uplifting divine souls."[4]

In order to understand Shri Vallabh, it is not enough to list the sites he visited or to hear of the miracles he performed. He did not consider magical acts important. The real attainment he taught was to become the Lord's unconditional follower. He even referred to himself as *Krishna Das* – the servant of Shri Krishna. He promoted the path of selfless, unconditional surrender to the Beloved of the Gopis, Shri Krishna.

Beloved Vallabh saw Shri Krishna as the essence of the Upanishads, comprised of pure nectar, unlimited, devoid of difference, the object of the Vedant, unattainable through meditation, who will yet happily appear and dance for His bhaktas. This lovely Krishna is ineffable, yet described by His lovers. He is unseen, yet appears before those who burn with joyous rapture.

For the benefit of ignited souls, Shri Vallabhacharya spent more than fifteen years of his life in three circumambulations of the Indian continent, accompanied by a small group of followers. He was known as "The one who is surrounded by other accomplished devotional adepts."[5]

Even now we can get glimpses of Shri Vallabh through the words of His disciple Padmanabhdas, a great scholar and bhakta:

Vallabh is a wearing a saffron-colored shawl and dhoti.
His forehead is graced with a tilak.
Auspicious mudras line his body.
From head to toe, his beauty is so great
that a billion love-gods are vanquished
by his sheer loveliness.
Those who were able to see him
were truly fortunate....
Then it was the sound of Krishna's flute –
Now it is the words of my beloved Vallabh.
He has left everything
to find and re-establish his divine souls.

Many people along the way did not agree with the young Vallabh, but after hearing his divine wisdom words, they left their shallow thoughts and turned towards his lotus feet. He became known as "The one with brilliant logic."[6] Many of those who came to dispute his views became his followers.

There are eighty-four seats, called *baithaks,* spread across the Indian subcontinent where the master resided for any number of days, often teaching his followers the Shrimad Bhagavatam, the most exalted text on the yoga of devotion. Shrines have been established at most of these seats. He went to these places to infuse the eternal dharma with a new life and to himself remain, as his son Shri Vitthalnathji has said, "Totally immersed in the nectar of Krishna's lilas."[7] Again, let us turn to his bhaktas to understand Shri Vallabh. Gopaldas sings:

He manifested upon this earth
*   with immeasurable brilliance and purity.*
*   He is both the sun and the moon.*
On the pretense of pilgrimage,
*   Shri Vallabh was spiritually victorious in every direction.*
He uplifted all the holy places
*   with the dust that touched his feet.[8]*

After his father's passing at Shri Balaji's temple, Shri Vallabh set out on his first pilgrimage from the north towards South India. He was eleven years old. The south was then comparatively free from Muslim dominance and religious disturbance. Shri Vallabh was a South Indian Brahmin, after all, and South India had a long tradition of learning and piety. His wanderings through Krishna's creation eventually brought him to the forests of Chitrakuta, where Lord Ram lived in exile with his wife Sita and brother Lakshman. The bhakti master found the world full of Brahman, a play of His names and forms, and honored every incarnation and sage that promoted the truth of eternal dharma.

From there Shri Vallabh moved on to his birth place, Champaranya, where he gave teachings on the Shrimad Bhagavatam. The dates and routes the Beloved took may not be exact, but they always reached deep into the heart of the land and people of India. We find the accounts of Shri Vallabh's travels in a book written by his grandson, Shri Gokulnathji, called the *Eighty-four Seats of Vallabhacharya.* Shri Gokulnathji noted many of the events in the master's life, and each account presents another level of understanding into Shri Vallabhacharya's life and mission.

In Mangalprashta, Dhondhi came to argue that the path of sacrifice was the supreme way. When the young Vallabh explained to him that pure devotion to God is the supreme path, Dhondhi attained wisdom and bowed at the master's feet. From there, Shri Vallabh went to Kundipura. At Balaji's temple in South India, Ravinath tested Shri Vallabh's knowledge of Vedic mantras. To his surprise, not only did Shri Vallabh correctly recite hundreds of mantras from the beginning to the end of the text, but he also recited them in reverse order! Wherever he went, Shri Vallabh revealed Shri Krishna's truth and refuted all other mayic theories that contradicted the true spirit of the Upanishads. Shri Vallabh became known as, "The one who explained the teaching of *Brahmavada*, where everything is Brahman and nothing but Brahman."[9]

The Beloved extracted the essence of all teachings and wherever he went, implanted a divine view in the minds and hearts of the people. He always retreated to isolated places and became known as a "lover of solitude."[10] In the inner recesses of the world and the heart, he contemplated the movements of the Beloved of the Gopis. He understood Shri Krishna's inner essence and passed that priceless gift on to others. No qualified person was barred from his path of loving devotion. He was the uplifter of all and gave his followers something even beyond liberation and enlightenment: Shri Krishna's nectar.

VIJAYNAGAR

While visiting the great Balaji temple during his first pilgrimage, Shri Vallabh heard about a conference at Vijaynagar, a stronghold of Vedic dharma. A controversial debate between the followers of Shri Shankar Acharya and the Vaishnavites of Shri Madhva Acharya had been going on for some time. Considering it his duty to uphold the devotional view, Shri Vallabh set out for this great southern Vedic kingdom, where his uncle held a position as King Krishnadeva's high priest. Even though he was only eleven years old, Vallabh was allowed to participate in the debate. Vyas Tirth presided over the discussion.

Despite his age, Shri Vallabh's view was spiritually mature. He based his teachings on the Vedas, Brahmasutra, Upanishads, Gita, as well as the Shrimad Bhagavatam, explaining that "Gayatri is the seed, the Vedas are the tree and the Bhagavat is the fruit." The Bhagavat contains the lilas of Shri Krishna and is therefore most beloved to him. Shri Vallabh was a non-dualist like Shankara but did not accept Shri Shankar's view of a false universe. He refuted the idea that souls are unreal and merely a product of maya. He felt as if Shri Shankar and his followers had appeared upon the stage of the world to proclaim that the play is false. If the stage is false, then so are the players, as well as what they say. Their non-dualism was mixed with maya and did not reflect the true non-dualism of the ageless Vedant. Furthermore, it was not conducive to devotion.

Shri Vallabh also differed with Shri Ramanuja's Vishistadvaita philosophy which holds the universe and the soul to be Brahman's qualities. Shri Vallabh saw everything as a pure part and parcel of Brahman, full of existence and consciousness. Shri Vallabh also countered the great Vaishnava Acharya Shri Madhva. Shri Madhva was a dualist and accepted Brahman as a creator, yet considered the universe and the soul to be different from Brahman. Vallabh saw only unqualified Brahman everywhere he looked.

Shri Vallabh explained to the assembled Vedic practitioners in front of King Krishnadeva, "The Upanishads teach a pure non-dual view. This is the correct view of Brahman and is in concordance with all scriptures. Brahman is real in every form. Maya is not in objects; it is the result of faulty perception, like when a dizzy person sees a stable pot spinning. The pot is real, but the spinning aspect of the pot is a product of maya – it is an illusion. In a similar way, the world is a perfect result, and maya arises when we do not see it properly. Maya misconstrues the view of the ideal real world. To consider the world as false or mayic is contrary to the spirit of the Vedant. The only time the world is ever mentioned as being mayic is to enforce a sense of detachment from worldliness in the practitioners. Otherwise it is quite clear that the world is Brahman's creation. It is only ignorance that makes it appear otherwise.

"Understand my point with reference to the Ganges River. She has three forms, all of which are real. One form of the Ganges is comprised of water; the second is a holy place of pilgrimage, while the third form of the Ganges is the divine goddess. The physical River Ganges is seen by all. Her holy aspect is known to those who have faith and knowledge, while her goddess form is known only to those who love her and perceive the unity among her physical water form, her holy pilgrimage aspect, and her divine form. In a similar way, Brahman has three forms. Brahman manifests as the world, as the unmanifested source of creation (the goal of the Yogi's abstract meditation), and as the divine Krishna, who is known by those who have attained not only wisdom, but a firm and all-encompassing love that is felt in every atom of creation. For them alone Krishna appears everywhere.[11]

"The followers of Shri Shankar have distorted the Vedant in order to popularize their own theory, which actually follows certain Buddhist views and not the pure teachings of the Upanishads. The Upanishads claim, 'This is all Brahman' and inspire us when they reveal, 'He is comprised of pure nectar. Whoever knows this becomes fearless.' Brahman manifests creation because Brahman did not feel totally complete until He became many. Brahman is devoid of difference, unlimited.

"When Brahman is formless, His joy is almost perfect, but understand that Brahman's essential form is Shri

Krishna, comprised of perfect truth, consciousness and bliss. When knowledge of Brahman is mixed with all-encompassing love, it becomes devotion. This is the way to liberation. Impure water that joins the Ganga becomes the Ganga and is no longer considered as pure or impure, but as sacred Ganga; similarly, everything that is offered to Brahman becomes Brahman.[12] After understanding the meaning of scriptures, serious practitioners should serve Shri Krishna with their minds, bodies and speech. Dedication is the way."

Hearing the young Vallabh's enlightening words, the entire court rose in applause and offered him the highest seat of honor. He was given the title Acharya, and from that day he was known as Shri Vallabhacharya. He was hailed for his great learning and clarity of thought. The king stood up and bowed to him. Shri Vallabh was declared victorious.

In honor of his victory, King Krishnadeva anointed the young Bhakti Master with water from golden vessels and then presented him with many kilos of gold. Shri Vallabh took only seven coins and distributed the rest to other Brahmins. He later used the seven coins to make ornaments for Shri Krishna. Shri Vallabhacharya stayed and gave teachings in Vijayanagar for about one year. Vyas Tirth requested him to become head of the Madhva lineage, but he humbly declined. Gopaldas sings of the event,

King Krishnadeva honored Shri Vallabhacharya with a golden bath
and four thousand kilos of gold.
Shri Vallabh quickly took leave of his palace
without even looking back upon the gold.[13]

FIRST PILGRIMAGE

Shri Vallabhacharya was offered fame and power at Vijayanagar, but his interests were non-worldly; he was inspired to continue his pilgrimage to bless the land and people of India. Shri Vallabhacharya visited Pampa Sarovar, a place sacred to Lord Ram. It was there that the low-caste Shabari offered berries to Lord Ram after tasting them first to make sure they were ripe. When Lord Ram accepted her half-eaten offerings, He demonstrated to the world how simple loving devotion can win the grace of God. Pure devotion that sways God's heart is a repeated theme in Shri Vallabhacharya's Path of Grace. The bhakti master himself explains in his *Shri Subodhini*,

We do not believe that a reward as excellent as Krishna can be attained through effort or practice.
In the light of grace, prescribed practices are inadequate.

Shri Vallabhacharya then continued on to Kumarapada, where the yogi Kapalika boasted of his yogic powers, "I can stop the motions of the sun and moon."

Shri Vallabhacharya calmly replied, "I will believe in your powers if you can get up from your seat."

When Kapalika could not even stir from his position, he requested Shri Vallabhacharya to withdraw his magical power. The master told him, "I am not aware of any magical power. The only power I have is the name of God. Give up your miraculous powers and believe only in the power of Shri Krishna."

Shri Mahaprabhu Vallabhacharya continued to teach his Path of Grace in many places. At Agala, a place associated with Shri Ramanujacharaya, he was given a warm welcome. He addressed an audience on the nature of Brahmavada, the

teaching that holds everything as purely Krishna. In Vishnu
Kanchi, at the well-known shrine of Shri Varadeswara, Shri
Vallabhacharya refused to climb the steps that went up to the
shrine because they were inscribed with Sanskrit verses from
Jayadeva's Ashtapadi, all in praise of Shri Krishna's Lila. The
head priest then arranged for the Bhakti Master to enter the
sanctum from another side.

Shri Vallabhacharya's respect for Krishna's name and
form was at the center of his teachings. He taught his
disciples, "If one is attached to Shri Krishna's seva, or to
hearing and reciting His names, stories and teachings, I
believe that as long as that bhakta lives, her devotion will
never be destroyed."[14]

Shri Vallabhacharya's Path of Grace is contagious
devotion. He taught his followers, "Remember your
dedication in the company of other accomplished bhaktas."[15]
Satsang, the holy association with other bhaktas, is the direct
path. People from all over India flocked to Shri
Vallabhacharya to experience his enlightened association.

Incidents in the master's life always turned into
teachings. At Padma Tirth, the king asked Shri
Vallabhacharya to cure his queen, who was possessed by an
evil spirit. Shri Vallabhacharya instructed his beloved
disciple Damodardas to give her some sacred earth from
Vrindavan mixed with water. The evil spirit left her as soon
as she took it. Shri Vallabhacharya then explained to the king,
"Faith in God is the only protection against evil spirits. They
can never enter a devotee."

His South Indian tour continued to Udupi, the
birthplace of Shri Madhvacharya, and then to Gokarna,
before returning to Vijayanagar, where he reunited with his
mother and other relatives. The king and queen requested
Shri Vallabh to settle down in their kingdom, but his desire
to pilgrimage to the North, the eventual seat of his devotion,

spurred him onwards. Other places he visited in South India during his first pilgrimage included Varkala, where Lord Janardhan left His temple to attend Shri Vallabhacharya's teachings, as well as Shri Rangan, Mount Malayachal, and the ashram of the sage Kaudinya.

DIVINE COMMANDS

In the year 1493 CE, on the eleventh day during the bright half of the month of Phalgun, Shri Krishna appeared to Shri Vallabhacharya in Jharakanda and told him, "I have appeared as Shri Nathji in a cave on the Govardhan Hill in North India. I am waiting for you to come before I emerge completely from the Hill. Quickly come here and perform My seva. There are some souls here in Vraj left over from the days of My Krishna avatar. Take them in your shelter. Only then will I agree to play with them. I will meet you on top of the Govardhan Hill."

After hearing Shri Nathji's command, Shri Vallabhacharya set out from Jharakanda for Vraj. While making his way north, he visited the famous temple of Shri Vitthal in Pandharpur, Maharashtra and received a special message that was to decide the future direction of his Path of Grace. Shri Krishna, appearing as Lord Vitthal, told Shri Vallabhacharya, "You are a great Acharya, not an ascetic. As a householder you will preach your message of love more effectively than as an ascetic. It is My wish that you marry. When an offer of matrimony comes to you, accept it. Name your younger son after Me." Gopaldas sings of that special occasion:

From there he went south to Pandu Rang
*   to Lord Krishna's Shri Vitthal temple.*

There, his eyes met Hari's
and through a silent gaze he asked,
"Give me your words."
He then spoke with the Lord of Shri,
Who said with certainty,
"It is My wish to become your son, Shri Vitthalnathji.
Become my father."
Krishna will now appear as Shri Vitthalnathji.
His form is a treasure. His eyes are like the lotus,
filled with numerous divine moods.
He will be worshipped by bhaktas in many lands.[16]

Shri Vallabhacharya then continued north to Nasik, Tranbaka and then on to Ujjain, shedding light on the Path of Grace wherever he went. Finally the young Vallabh reached his beloved land of Vraj, Shri Krishna's land of Lila. He first went to Mathura and bathed in the Yamuna River at Vishranti Ghat. His entrance into Vraj, Shri Krishna's circle of twelve forests, would further enhance the direction and scope of his divine mission. He chose a Brahmin Chaube named Ujagar to assist him in Vraj, and in Mathura he gave a discourse on the Shrimad Bhagavatam.

One day, as Shri Vallabhacharya was going to Vishranti Ghat in Mathura to take his bath, Ujagar Chaube informed him, "The Emperor's minister, Rustamalli came to Mathura and got angry with the local Brahmins. He had a charm attached to the gate by Vishranti Ghat, where a Muslim guard sits. Any Hindu who passes under the gate loses his *shika* (a small ponytail of hair worn by Hindus), and immediately grows a Muslim style beard. That spell has stopped all Hindus from bathing at the ghat."

Shri Mahaprabhuji then created his own charm on a piece of paper and told his disciples Vasudevadas and Krishnadas, "Go to Delhi and attach this charm to the main gate there." When they attached Shri Vallabhacharya's charm to the main gate, any Muslim that walked beneath it lost his beard and suddenly grew a Hindu shika ponytail.

The Emperor, Sikandar Lodi, heard of the troublesome spell and summoned Vasudevadas and Krishnadas. When they explained the entire situation to the Emperor, he immediately had the spell removed from Mathura and told Rustamalli, "Don't be so intimidated by petty taunts."

Shri Vallabhacharya rarely demonstrated any supernatural powers, for he only believed in devotional powers. When he went to the Yamuna River, he bowed his head happily before the divine Goddess Yamuna and sang her praises: "I joyfully bow to you Shri Yamuna! You are the holder of all divine powers."

The Bhakti Master was not interested in the manipulation of matter, but in the transformation of being, so that the sensitive bhakta-lover could strengthen her love for Shri Krishna, allowing her to participate in His love games and feel His Presence everywhere. Shri Vallabhacharya explains in his Shri Subodhini, "Only Hari can cause the awakening. It occurs after the experiences of renunciation, knowledge, yoga, austerity and devotion."

Renunciation in the Path of Grace does not embrace any negativity towards the world. It is spontaneous, derived from unflinching love and devotion to Shri Krishna. It is through all-encompassing love that other attachments are naturally shed without a trace of resentment.

Knowledge for these blessed bhaktas appears when they have the intuitive and direct experience of Shri Krishna's divine form. Yoga is not a meditative exercise, but a one-pointed yoking of the heart and mind directly to Shri Krishna. It is not based upon any practice, but upon Krishna.

Tapa, or austerity is perfected when one feels Shri Krishna's presence and then His separation. Separation is a result of direct contact with Brahman. Separation is Krishna in the heart, while union is Krishna in the world. Know that union and separation are the two sides of the single petal of love.

When there is devotion, all other pursuits are naturally renounced, including the desire for liberation or enlightenment. What is there to be liberated from when the Lord of enlightenment chases after His bhaktas?

Beloved Vallabh admired Shri Yamuna's waters, made fragrant by flowers from the lovely forests that graced her banks, and dark like Krishna, with expansive sands shining bright like Krishna's lotus feet. He felt that Shri Yamuna contains the splendor of Shri Krishna. This inspired the master to follow her waters downstream a few kilometers to Gokul.

BRAHMA SAMBANDHA

Shri Vallabhacharya reached Gokul on the eleventh day of the bright phase of the moon during the month of Shravan (August) in 1494 CE. At that time the master's mind was concerned with the upliftment of divine souls. He had noticed that people were spiritually divided. Vedic rituals had lost their significance and mantras were mostly ineffective. In such a time, he thought, "What will be the fate of the blessed ones?"

He took rest that evening on Thakurani Ghat by the banks of the Yamuna River. At midnight the Blessed Lord Krishna personally appeared to him. The following morning, Shri Vallabhacharya wrote about his divine experience and the teachings he received from the Blessed Lord in Sanskrit. In the Master's own words:

"At midnight on the eleventh lunar day during the bright half of the month of Shravan, Shri Krishna appeared before me. I will now reveal the words He spoke. Shri Krishna explained to me that after taking Brahma Sambandha and thereby establishing a connection to Brahman, the impurities of the soul are completely removed. These impurities are said to be of five kinds. As explained in Vedic and worldly texts, these five impurities are natural impurities as well as those related to time, place, association and physical contact. After taking Brahma Sambandha, they should no longer be considered valid. These impurities can never be removed without connection to Brahman. Therefore anything that has not been offered to the Lord should not be used. Dedicated souls should perform all activities by first offering them to the Blessed Lord. This is the way a bhakta should always live. Anything that has been previously enjoyed should never be offered to Shri Krishna, the Supreme Lord of all the devas. Therefore, at the start of any undertaking, everything should first be dedicated to Him. The statement that says, 'It is all His and therefore cannot be used,' holds no validity here and refers to another path. Just like good servants in the world are known for their selfless service, the bhakta selflessly offers herself in every undertaking, and then everything becomes divine for her. Like impure water that joins the Ganga becomes the Ganga and is no longer considered as pure or impure, but as sacred Ganga, similarly, everything that is offered to the Lord becomes like Him – perfectly divine."[17]

Shri Krishna then conferred upon his Beloved Vallabh the *Brahma Sambandha mantra* with which to initiate his disciples, Shri Krishna's own divine souls. This initiation would enable them to consecrate their lives by reestablishing their forgotten connection (*sambandha*) with the Divine (*Brahma*). Still today, this initiation is given by the lineage

holders of the Path of Grace, Shri Vallabh's descendants.
Those who receive the Brahma Sambandha initiation become
eligible to perform Shri Krishna's seva, His loving service.
Its English translation is given below.

The Brahma Sambandha Mantra

*"Thousands of years have passed in separation from You, and I am
filled with intense pain and anguish. I have lost my true joy and
now dedicate my body, senses, vital breath, mind, intelligence,
reason and sense of self along with all their functions, as well as
my spouse, children, house, relatives, and wealth in this world or
any other, along with my soul, to You, Shri Krishna. Shri Krishna,
I am yours."*

The following morning Shri Vallabh asked his closest
disciple, Damala, who was sleeping next to him, "Did you
hear the Lord speaking to me last night?"

Damala replied, "One can hear a lot in life, but if even
celestial speech is unintelligible, how could one understand
the utterances of the Supreme Being? I will only understand
when you shower your grace and explain. I perceive that you
have met your beloved Lord, but what more can this humble
servant understand?"

In this way Damala showed his devotion and
humility before Shri Vallabhacharya and set the perfect
example for other followers of grace. Shri Vallabhacharya
then initiated him with the mantra Shri Krishna had given,
and Damala became the first disciple of the Path of Grace.

PRATHAM MILAN:
FIRST MEETING

Remembering what Shri Nathji had told him in South India, Shri Mahaprabhu Vallabhacharya then proceeded from Gokul to the Govardhan Hill and reached Saddu Pande's house in Anyor. Many local *Vrajvasis* came to see him and thought, "He is truly a great soul."

Suddenly, Shri Vallabhacharya overheard Shri Nathji calling out from on top of the Govardhan Hill to Saddu Pande's daughter, "O, Naro! Bring Me some milk."

Naro replied, "Today we have a guest."

"That is great, but could you please bring Me some milk?"

After offering Shri Nathji milk, she brought down the bowl containing some of His leftover milk. Shri Vallabhacharya said, "Please give me some of that leftover milk."

Naro replied, "Maharaja, we have plenty of milk in the house. Take as much as you like."

"I am not interested in any other milk, only what is in that bowl."

Saddu Pande then told Shri Vallabhacharya all about Shri Nathji's appearance, and the Bhakti Master's heart overflowed with joy. The following day, Shri Vallabhacharya joyfully climbed up the Govardhan Hill, where Shri Nathji greeted him with a warm embrace. This divine moment of their 'first meeting,' or *Pratham Milan*, is a frequently depicted scene in Pushti Marg artwork. Shri Vallabhacharya then established Shri Nathji's daily worship on top of the Govardhan Hill, for without seva, there is no entrance into the Path of Grace.

Nearby, at Apsara Lake, there is a cave where the great bhakta Ramdas lived. After Ramdas became his disciple, Shri Mahaprabhuji told him, "Perform Shri Nathji's seva."

"I don't know anything about seva," said Ramdas.

"Don't worry. Shri Nathji will teach you," the guru replied.

Shri Mahaprabhuji then had a peacock feather crown prepared and made Shri Nathji's ornamentation. He later instructed Ramdas in the arts of seva and explained to him, "Every day after you bathe in the Govinda Lake, take a pot of water and bathe Shri Nathji. Then dress Him in clothes just as I have done. Adorn Shri Nathji with a peacock feather crown and a gunja bead necklace. Whatever foods you are able to attain, through His wish, prepare and offer them to Shri Nathji. The Vraj residents will bring you their milk and curds."

Shri Mahaprabhuji then told Saddu Pande and the other Vraj residents, "Shri Nathji is my all and everything. Remain attached to His seva, and be ever ready to react to any complication. Most importantly, keep Shri Nathji happy."

Then Shri Vallabhacharya prepared an offering of cooked grains with his own hands. Until that day, Shri Nathji had only taken milk and curds. After Shri Vallabhacharya cooked Shri Nathji His first meal, the Blessed Lord started to grab food from the Vrajvasis' lunch boxes as they went out to herd their cows.

In the year 1499 CE, during the second day of the bright half of the month of Chaitra, Shri Nathji appeared in Purnamal's dream and told him, "Come to Vraj and build a large temple for Me."

Purnamal gathered his wealth, left his town of Ambalya and travelled to the Govardhan Hill, where Shri Mahaprabhuji gave him permission, "Yes, quickly build the temple."

Shri Mahaprabhuji then directly asked the Govardhan Hill if He would mind a temple being constructed upon His sacred stones. The Govardhan Hill replied, "Shri Nathji always resides in My heart. I will not be troubled. Construct the temple, with pleasure."

When a design was prepared for Shri Nathji's temple, Shri Mahaprabhu Vallabhacharya saw the temple towers and told the designer, Hiramani to make another plan without towers. When the second design also included two towers, Shri Mahaprabhuji told Hiramani to make a third design without towers. When the third design came, still showing temple towers, Shri Mahaprabhuji told Damodardas, "It must be Shri Nathji's wish to have a temple with towers on it. Shri Nathji will stay in this temple for a while, but when conflict with the Mughals arises, Shri Nathji will move west to Rajasthan."

It was Shri Nathji's wish that His temple be built with its towers and seen by all. Shri Vallabhacharya preferred to live in isolation, but Shri Nathji is the Uplifter not only of divine souls, but of all souls. For the time being, Shri Nathji played with His local bhaktas and waited twenty years for His temple to be finally completed. Then Shri Mahaprabhuji returned to Vraj and established Shri Nathji in His new temple, on the third day of the bright half of the month of Vaishaka, in the year 1519 CE.

Shri Vallabhacharya loved to live in Shri Krishna's land of Vraj. Mahaprabhuji's followers called him, "The One who adores Vraj."[18] Shri Krishna's lilas, the focus of Shri Vallabhacharya's teachings, can easily be felt in the sacred forests of Vrindavan. Shri Vallabhacharya reveled there in Shri Krishna's constant divine presence.

After Shri Nathji began to reside in His new temple, Shri Vallabhacharya blessed Purnamal, "Ask anything you desire of me."

Purnamal replied, "I would like to offer Shri Nathji some very fine sandalwood paste with my own hands."

"Happily make your offering," Mahaprabhuji consented.

Shri Mahaprabhuji adorned Shri Nathji with clothes and ornaments on that day, and there was a huge festival. The joy experienced by all was ineffable. Afterwards, Shri Mahaprabhuji made his disciple Krishnadas the temple manager and Kumbhandas became the temple singer. Shri Mahaprabhuji told them what foods should be offered to Shri Nathji daily, and Saddu Pande made sure that the necessary ingredients were delivered to the temple.

On the day before Shri Mahaprabhuji was going to leave, Shri Nathji told him, "I want a cow."

"I will arrange for one," Mahaprabhuji replied.

Shri Vallabhacharya then told Saddu Pande, "Shri Nathji wants a cow. Sell this gold ring of mine and purchase a cow for Shri Nathji with the money."

Saddu Pande replied, "I have so many cows and buffaloes. They are all yours. Just tell me how many cows you want."

"If you give your cows to Shri Nathji, then I have not truly given Him any. So sell my ring and purchase a cow for Shri Nathji," Mahaprabhuji insisted.

Saddu Pande purchased a cow and brought her before Shri Nathji. He was very pleased. When the Vrajvasis heard that Shri Nathji loves cows, one by one they all began to offer Shri Nathji cows. Someone gave Shri Nathji four cows, and someone else gave Him eight. Many people gifted Shri Nathji cows, and His herd grew into the thousands. Shri Mahaprabhuji started to call Shri Nathji, "Gopal." The bhakta poet Chitaswami sang of Shri Nathji and His cows:

In front of Him there are cows.
In back of Him there are cows.
Here are cows and there are cows.
Govinda loves to live among His cows.
He runs with His cows.
He is content with His cows.
He anoints His body with the dust
raised by the hooves of the cows.
When the cows cover Vraj, one forgets
the eternal realm of Vaikuntha.
Mountain Holder Krishna, who has appeared as Vitthalnathji,
is coming home with His cows in the garb of a cowlad.

VRAJ LILAS

After arranging Shri Nathji's temple affairs, the bhakti master went to Vrindavan. The bhakta Gopaldas sings of that Lila realm,

Where black bees buzz, and the trees, flowers and jasmine buds
perfume the air with unlimited fragrance,
a delightful Shyam Tamal tree blossoms
with clusters of iridescent flowers.
In Vrindavan, the blessed Swaminis please Krishna
with their lovely, lilting movements and gestures.
Upon hearing the divine notes and sounds,
the sages, appearing as Vrindavan peacocks,
fall into meditative trance as they imbibe
the nectar of the endless Lila.
Boundless radiance engulfs the lovely Lila abode.
Krishna delights there, playing in diverse Rasa Lila circles.

After arriving in the divine area of Vrindavan, Shri Vallabhacharya offered some *prasad* to his disciple

Prabhudas, who said, "I cannot accept this now, as I haven't bathed yet."

Shri Vallabhacharya explained, "In this sacred land of Vrindavan, Shri Krishna lives within every leaf, playing a lovely melody on His flute. In such a place, where every grain of sand is sacred, why consider whether you have bathed or not?" When Prabhudas turned towards the trees, he saw Shri Krishna's face beaming in every leaf and flower.

Shri Vallabhacharya worshipped various forms of Vrindavan Krishna. Sometimes he worshipped Him as a child (Bal Krishna), as youthful Shri Nathji, or as Gokul Chandramaji – the flute playing "Moon of Gokul." Shri Vallabhacharya spoke to his followers about Vrindavan and his devotion to Shri Krishna:

"Krishna enters this magical forest of Vrindavan and awakens the divinities who reside there. He accomplishes this through the call of His flute. He has opened the gates of love, and the blessed women of Vraj are swept away in a current of *bhava* play with Him. This takes place very close to their homes here in Vrindavan. The lakes of Vraj, the Yamuna River and the adjoining hillsides are all abodes of divine dalliance. Krishna is ready to love and prepares others. Shri Krishna is love's personified form. The Vraj Gopis nourish that love and inspire it to arise."

Shri Vallabhacharya is the perfect witness to Krishna's Lila and the Lord of speech. His words not only taught about divine experience, but created it as well. He continued to reveal the mysteries of Vrindavan:

"In order to awaken divine attachment, Hari enters Vrindavan playing His flute. The Gopis sang of Shri Krishna's flute song. Whoever is attracted to His attributes becomes attached to Him in the end."

The souls Shri Vallabhacharya accepted became beloveds of the Lord of the Gopis. He gave his eligible followers the direct experience of Shri Krishna and brought the divine realm of Vrindavan to this earth for them. He taught them that the highest reward was not to return to God, but to have God return to the soul here in this world. Human birth was not the result of negative karmas, but a supreme opportunity to have exchanges with Shri Krishna in this world, in one's own home. Shri Vallabhacharya's path reveals the way to dedicate everything, use it for Krishna's pleasure, and then to live on His prasad. To wear offered cloth and live in a totally offered world is not only the key to rise above all forms of anxiety, but the path to Presence. The search for the Beloved is a continual process. The Path of Grace is a fiery affair which revolves between the experiences of finding Shri Krishna in the world and then in the heart.

Beloved Vallabh's speech was Brahmic in every direction. Shri Vallabhacharya did not see Vrindavan, the sacred lands of Shri Krishna's lilas, as a pilgrimage destination, but rather as Shri Krishna's divine abode appearing in the world. He urged his followers to serve Shri Krishna, for wherever one makes Shri Krishna's seva becomes Vrindavan. To experience Krishna with all of one's senses is the highest reward of human life. True liberation is to make yourself so spiritually attractive that Shri Krishna can't wait to find you! In the Path of Grace, exalted souls find Shri Krishna everywhere they look, and there is a constant exchange.

Shri Vallabhacharya is brilliant at giving the unattainable gift: direct insight into the nature of Shri Krishna. Anywhere his lotus feet touched the ground became a non-dual divine realm. The bhakti master wandered the twelve forests of Vraj with a handful of dedicated followers. Vraj is the area with the highest concentration of *baithaks*, or 'seats,' temples dedicated to Shri Vallabhacharya where the Master taught Shri Krishna's divine essence as revealed in the Shrimad Bhagavat. In Vraj, as elsewhere, his mission was to awaken Shri Krishna's presence in the people he met. To his scribe, Kashmiri Bhatt and other intimate followers, he conveyed the inner mood of Vrindavan, as described by the Beloved Gopi dairymaids:

"We experience Krishna with our eyes. We feel Him through all of our senses. Hari is the desire, the festival of our hearts. To imbibe Krishna's form is the ultimate reward. To have conversations with the Beloved, to behold Him, to embrace Him – this is what we live for.

"We have heard the nectar of His flute and now savor His fragrance everywhere. We approach Krishna directly and stand in His joyful proximity. We integrate all of these *bhavas* (divine moods) continually into our devotion. Understand us. We know that the fruit of attaining human form is to use our God-given senses to experience God, to join them in Hari's pleasure. For us, to behold Him with eyes, or better yet, with all senses – to imbibe His form, His divine essence – that alone is the reward. We have no use for the liberation of merging into Brahman, where the ability to taste and discern Him is annihilated....If we merged with Hari, we would lose the opportunity to experience Him."

This intense devotion was not understood by all. Once, in Mathura, Sanatan Goswami approached Shri Vallabhacharya and said, "Yours is the Path of Grace, the path of nourishment, yet all of your followers are thin."

Shri Vallabhacharya turned to him and explained, "I told them not to come, but they came anyway. That is why they are thin."

Sanatan Goswami did not understand the master's reply. He later related Shri Vallabhacharya's words to his guru, Shri Krishna Chaitanya, who immediately fell to the ground in a divine swoon. When he arose several hours later, he again asked Sanatan what Shri Vallabhacharya had said.

Hearing the master's words a second time, he again fell unconscious. Shri Chaitanya understood that when Shri Vallabhacharya said, "I told them not to come," he was referring to a passage in the Shrimad Bhagavatam which describes Shri Krishna's forest Lila with the Gopis. When they first came to meet Him under the full moon in the Vrindavan forest, He told them to return home.

His comment, "They came anyway, and that is why they are thin," refers to the Gopis' divine condition. After Shri Krishna told them to go, they refused His advice and then enjoyed His divine company and dance. After their union with Shri Krishna, they returned home and experienced deep separation from their Blessed Lord, which made them thin. Shri Krishna Chaitanya truly took Shri Vallabhacharya's words to heart.

The Path of Grace embraces contradictions. Union is found in separation, intensity is mixed with humility, and the goal is never dependent on a particular practice; the practitioner depends on Shri Krishna alone. Master Vallabh was also very practical and understood the pitfalls of spiritual life. He taught that the only means to attain the blessed state is through humility coupled with overwhelming desire to come face to face with the Beloved. Pride of practice, anxiety and false expectations are all obstructions to attainment.

One day while wandering in Vraj, Shri Vallabh passed through the Gehvarvan forest, near Shri Radha's town of Barsana. There the master's attention was drawn to a large boa constrictor in a field. The snake was being consumed by ants. He was deeply moved by the sight and explained to his disciples, "In its previous birth, this snake was a false guru, a man who posed as an enlightened being. These ants are his disciples, whom he failed to uplift. Bhaktas always relinquish all sense of false pride and come humbly before the Blessed One. They adore Him with every sentiment, and if anxiety creeps into their lives for any reason, they realize it as His play and quickly relinquish all concerns.

"The Lord of all, Shri Krishna, will never enter the heart of one who is filled with worldly hankerings. Krishna comes before us when we sing His praises, full of devotion. That unmatched divine pleasure surpasses even liberation. That is why Shri Krishna brought His bhaktas to the land of Vrindavan – to free them from the abode of liberation. He came to Vrindavan to play and award them the pleasure of His divine being. Life, for the divine soul, is to enter His love plays and serve."

A very learned pandit named Padmanabhdas became Shri Vallabhacharya's disciple and joined him on pilgrimage to Vraj. Padmanabhdas was very intellectual and said he would only be convinced of Shri Krishna's personal divine reality if he could actually see the Blessed Lord. Shri Vallabhacharya, who provides all rewards, understood the desire of his heart. One day while they were walking near Gokul, a sand cliff in the banks of the Yamuna River broke apart, and out of it emerged an actual form of the Lord, as tall as an enormous tree. He came before Shri Acharyaji and commanded, "Perform My seva."

Shri Acharyaji replied, "Maharaj! These days Vaishnavas do not have the power to perform Your seva and ornamentation. If it is Your wish to accept worship from the Vaishnavas, then present Yourself such that You can sit in my lap." Shri Krishna then took a smaller form and sat in the Master's lap, with His head reaching just to Shri Mahaprabhuji's chin. Shri Mahaprabhuji named Him 'Shri Mathuranathji' and told Padmanabhdas, "Now perform Shri Krishna's seva and be content with whatever comes to you."

Souls established in grace see the Lord as full of grace. They appear in this world to serve His divine form. Their bodies become transformed and capable of attending to the Lord of Sweetness. As Shri Vallabhacharya, the knower of Krishna's heart, sang when he beheld Shri Krishna in the town of Gokul,

> *His lips are sweet.*
> > *His face is sweet.*
> *His eyes are sweet.*
> > *His laugh is sweet.*
> *His heart is sweet.*
> > *His movements are sweet.*
> *He is the Lord of sweetness,*
> > *and everything is totally sweet.*

The separated divine souls required the Master's touch to awaken their inner divinity before they could please the Lord of sweetness and feel His presence. Who besides the bhakta, the follower of the all blissful Hari, is able to relieve His burden? One day, while looking towards a Vrindavan cloud, Shri Vallabh explained to his intimate disciples:

"Look at that cloud. She was first moved by love, which increased when she heard Shri Krishna's glories. That love then matured into a fast friendship Him. Love inspired her to take form. Clouds are the forms of desire and can take on any shape at will. It was because of her great affection and the nature of Hari's play that she expanded and shaded Krishna and all of His friends as they played under the hot Vrindavan sun. She is never troubled by her efforts; rather, she is enthralled."

The bhakti master reflected, "One who can develop and cultivate devotion attains the blessed state of *atma-nivedanam:* soul dedication. This cloud has attained that perfect state of being. Some people compare that cloud to

Krishna, since she is "charitable like Hari. She also shares His hue and like Him, nourishes and helps create life with her waters."

His followers listened with rapt attention. The words of the Master of Speech brought them into total awareness of Krishna. He then continued, "Those who share similar qualities are generally friends. This cloud excels even in friendship. She has given everything she owns to Krishna. Her nectar essence of flowers is freely offered to Hari. It is an act of selfless love."

THE SECOND PILGRIMAGE

To expand the teachings of loving devotion, Shri Vallabhacharya left his beloved Vraj and began a second pilgrimage around India, first heading westward into Rajasthan. He stopped at Pushkar, a pilgrimage site sacred to Lord Brahma, to give teachings on the Shrimad Bhagavat. From there he entered Gujarat, where he taught at many places throughout the region and initiated many disciples. Even today, the greatest concentration of Pushti Marg followers is found in Gujarat. The bhakti master proceeded to Vadanagar, Visnagar, Kheralu, Dakor, and Broach. In Durvasa Shri Vallabhacharya met a man who was practicing severe penance and explained to him, "This is not the right way to attain the Supreme. You are torturing yourself. To understand the Lord, love is required. Devotion is the key. One can see the Lord by understanding and emulating the devotion of the great bhaktas."

Shri Vallabhacharya's great grandson, Shri Harirayaji, would later sing:

Fool, why are you harassing your body
with all these silly practices?

Missing the Bliss at hand,
you are running the wrong way!

From there Shri Vallabhacharya went to Bhanu, Kapisha and then Tagadi, where crowds flocked to him. There he spoke on the lilas of Lord Krishna and explained that children should be loved as images of God, just as Krishna's mother Yashoda loved her two sons Shri Krishna and Balaram. A Brahmin couple who attended the teachings later found their sons eating butter from the churning pot and called Shri Vallabhacharya to their house to show him their children's divine activities.

Shri Vallabhacharya insisted that his disciples should serve Shri Krishna's *svarupa*, (literally, His true divine form) and established Shri Krishna's seva in their homes. He initiated his followers into the modes of loving service and told them, "Always perform Shri Krishna's pleasing service, or *seva*. The highest form of seva is when it spontaneously fills the mind and heart. This state of being arises when one's consciousness is threaded into Krishna. In order to attain this state, bhaktas employ their bodies, together with their wealth, in Shri Krishna's beloved service. Then the pains of the world are removed and knowledge of Brahman arises."[19]

Shri Vallabhacharya then continued on his way, visiting Veraval and Junagarh and then Dwarka, where many followers of Shri Shankaracharya who came to debate with the bhakti master ended up becoming his disciples. Near Gopi Talaiy, the 'Gopi Lake,' Shri Mahaprabhu Vallabhacharya told his disciples the following story:

"Once, when Shri Krishna mentioned to Shri Rukminiji how He played the flute and called the Gopis out to dance in the forest of Vrindavan, Shri Rukmini remarked, 'I would like to experience that Rasa Lila!'

"Shri Krishna laughed and said, 'How will you make it out to the forest at night? You will not be able to renounce your worldly concerns like the Gopis of Vrindavan did.'

"'Just play Your flute and see,' she replied.

"Rukmini then returned to the palace and told all the other Dwarka Queens to adorn and ready themselves for Krishna's nighttime forest lila. Later that evening, Shri Krishna went to the Gopi Lake and played His flute. Hearing the call, Shri Rukminiji and other Dwarka Queens, along with their women associates and attendants, headed out of their palaces, everyone fully adorned. When they approached the main gates and saw their in-laws and senior family members there, they hesitated, 'What will we say if they ask us where we are going? We had better stay home tonight.'

"While the Queens retreated to their respectful palaces, Shri Krishna, Who was ready to dance, understood what had happened to the Queens and sounded His flute again to call the Gopis of Vraj. Out of Shri Krishna's sixteen thousand Dwarka queens, only five managed to get out of their palaces to experience the Lord's delightful grace filled form and His Vrindavan lila along with the Gopis."

Wherever Shri Vallabhacharya went, his presence was so powerful that the fragrance from his lotus feet was able to uplift even those souls who did not get close enough to see him! The Krishna deities residing in the temples where Shri Vallabhacharya visited would often appear in living form before the master. Sometimes they appeared to him when he visited their temples, and at other times they would visit his camp. It was an amazing time. Shri Vallabhacharya created a devotional renaissance wherever he went.

Shri Vallabhacharya taught even as he walked: "This creation is a lila, a divine play wherein every being is searching for its core of bliss. Since bliss is concealed, it must be discovered. For that bliss to be disclosed, wisdom enhanced with overwhelming love is required. Only then can blissful Brahman be found within all divine manifestations. Then the bhakta is able to truly experience life and flourish in a world where perceptible names and forms are perfectly contained within a holistic, non-dual experience."

Beloved Vallabh then turned toward the Himalayas and Hardvara, Kedarnath and Badrinath. In Badrinath he met the famous sage, Veda Vyas. In the sage's high Himalayan cave, they discussed the inner meanings of the Shrimad Bhagavatam. Returning to the plains, in Naimisharanya, Mahaprabhuji told his listeners that knowledge devoid of devotion is ineffectual, and that devotees should seek the Lord's grace through selfless love.

The bhakti master then proceeded to Ayodhya, Prayag, Benares, Harehar, Gaya, and then Ganga Sagar, where the sacred Ganges River meets the ocean. He stayed there for six months composing his commentary on the third canto of the Shrimad Bhagavatam. At Ganga Sagar, Shri Krishna appeared again to Shri Vallabhacharya and told him that it was time for him to complete his earthly mission and return to Him. Feeling that his work was incomplete, Shri Vallabhacharya declined the Lord's command and continued on to Jagannath Puri, where he was given some rice prasad on a fast day. Not wanting to disrespect to the offering, nor break his fast by eating the grain, he stood for the entire night in the temple, singing the praises of food that has been offered to Shri Krishna. When the sun rose on the following day, marking the end of his fast, he ate the blessed rice prasad.

Later the king of Jagannath Puri questioned Shri Vallabhacharya, "Who is the highest deity? What is the main scripture and the most holy mantra? Finally, what is the most exalted work we can do?"

The bhakti master put these questions onto a piece of paper, placed it in the inner temple, and closed the doors.

He awaited the Lord's response. When the temple opened, each question had been precisely answered in Sanskrit by Lord Jagannath:

> *Know that the Bhagavat Gita is the main scripture. Lord Krishna is the Lord of lords. His name is the highest mantra, and no work surpasses His service.*

MARRIAGE AND THIRD PILGRIMAGE

From the coast of eastern India, Shri Vallabhacharya returned to Benares and accepted Mahalakshmi as his wife. The master spent many years in Benares and composed many devotional works for his disciples. Govinda Dube once approached his guru and said that he was unable to focus his mind on Shri Krishna's seva, because he was plagued with anxiety. Shri Vallabhacharya composed a teaching called the *Nine Jewels* for him, in which the master explained:

"Those who have dedicated their very selves should never worry, because the Blessed Lord, Who is established in grace, will never give them a mundane life....The Supreme Being, Shri Krishna, the Self of all, will do as He pleases and will fulfill His bhakta's desires....If those who have dedicated themselves with or without proper understanding should have no concerns, then what to say of those who have established their very life-force with Krishna? Concerns regarding one's dedication, as well as anxieties regarding any other involvements in life, should be given over to Shri Krishna. These worries should be renounced, because Hari Himself is totally capable of taking care of His own bhaktas....Therefore, with total love, feel Shri Krishna everywhere and continually recite, 'Shri Krishna is my refuge.' This is my firm conviction."

Govinda Dube's anxieties were removed when he heard these teachings. Shri Vallabhacharya's third and last pilgrimage through India lasted four years. He revisited many of the places he had been to on his first and second pilgrimages. Everywhere he went, he was hailed as the greatest teacher of his time. Among his disciples were kings, yogis, Muslims, the rich and the poor. Through the intervention of Shri Vallabhacharya and their own soulful dedication, every true disciple obtained the grace of the Lord.

It was perhaps during Shri Mahaprabhuji's third visit to Vraj that the great blind poet, Surdas came before the bhakti master by the banks of the Yamuna, just south of Mathura at Go Ghat. Surdas had already created a large following of his own but humbly came before Shri Vallabhacharya. Having heard of Surdas' poetic and musical skill, Shri Vallabhacharya requested, "Surdas, sing something about Shri Krishna's Lila." Surdas sang,

> *I am the king of all sinners.*
> *Others may have sinned a few times,*
> > *but I have committed sin after sin*
> > *from my very birth.*

Hearing Surdas' poem, Shri Mahaprabhuji remarked, "How is it that Sur, whose name means, 'warrior,' whimpers thus? I asked you to praise the glories of Shri Krishna, not sing about your own shortcomings!"

Surdas then humbly admitted, "I know nothing of Hari's lilas."

Shri Mahaprabhuji turned to him and said, "Go now and bathe in the Yamuna River. When you return, I will explain them to you." After Surdas had bathed and returned cleansed to the bhakti master, Shri Mahaprabhuji graced him with *Ashtakshara mantra* ('Shri Krishna is my refuge') and then completed Surdas' dedication by initiating him with the Brahma Sambandha mantra. After Shri Mahaprabhuji gave Surdas total knowledge of the secret devotional teachings found in his Shri Subodhini text, the divine lilas arose clearly in Surdas' heart. Shri Mahaprabhuji wrote in the 'mangalacharan' introduction to the 10th canto section of Shri Subodhini, "I bow to Shri Krishna, an ocean of divine potency. He resides within the limitless heart, in a milky and nectarine ocean of divine plays, where He is served by thousands of Lakshmis, all engaged in His Lila."

Surdas then sang before the great master the following poem, in accordance with that line:

> *Chakai bird!*
> *Fly now to the reservoir of the Lord's feet,*
> > *where there is no separation from love –*
> > *where the oblivion of darkness never prevails.*
> *It is a sea of joyous union.*
> *Sings Surajadas,*
> *"Now, I have no taste for anything petty.*
> > *My hopes lie in that lake."*

As Surdas' heart opened, the lilas of Shri Krishna gushed into him and allowed the blind poet to witness Shri Krishna's appearance. He then sang before Shri Vallabhacharya, "When the people and singers of Gokul heard that Nanda was the father of a newborn son, Shri Krishna, their joy was boundless."

By the guru's grace, Lord Krishna had now appeared to the blind poet. As he witnessed Shri Krishna's appearance in Gokul, Surdas described the divine event at great length. When he was about to sing about the intimate love the Gopis felt for Shri Krishna, Shri Vallabhacharya stopped him in the middle of his verse and himself sang, "O, listen Sur!

Everyone who worships Lord Krishna's feet will reach that destiny."

Shri Vallabhacharya interrupted Surdas' song because he did not want the blind bhakti-poet to reveal the inner lilas before all the people present there. The bliss of the Vraj bhaktas, the Gopis, is something to be experienced in the hearts of great devotees. Shri Mahaprabhuji stopped Surdas from revealing that intimate love outwardly. Shri Vallabhacharya also quelled Surdas' doubt that, 'I have made all these disciples. What will become of them?' by promising that they too would attain if they were to dedicate themselves at Shri Krishna's feet.

Surdas went on to sing thousands of poems in praise of Child Krishna, as well as Shri Radha and Krishna, in front of Shri Nathji on the Govardhan Hill. He composed 100,000 poems and ascribed the inspiration behind all of his writing to his Beloved Vallabh. On his death bed he sang,

> *I have firm faith in Shri Vallabh's lotus feet.*
> *Without the moonbeams that shine from His toenails,*
> *the entire world falls into darkness.*
> *In this age of struggle, there is no other practice*
> *by which to attain true liberation*
> *Sings Sur, I may be blind in two ways,*
> *but I am His priceless servant.*

ADEL AND BEYOND

From Vraj, Shri Vallabhacharya returned home to Benares, where he devoted his time to seva and experiencing the joys of Shri Krishna. In Benares, many of the followers of Shri Shankaracharya were hostile towards Shri Mahaprabhu Vallabhacharya and his devotional views. To silence them, Shri Vallabhacharya wrote a text called

Patravalamban, which he placed on the wall of the main Shiva
temple. It explained that the Vedic texts which address action
as well as those which reveal knowledge are completely
complimentary. Still, the bhakti master desired to live in
peace and shifted his residence from Benares to Adel, a quiet
residence at the confluence of the Ganga and Yamuna Rivers,
facing Prayag.

In 1512 CE, Mahaprabhuji's first son, Gopinathji, was
born in Adel, and in 1516 his second son, Shri Vitthalnathji
was born in Charanat, near Benares. Gopinathji's lineage did
not continue beyond his only son. Shri Vitthalnathji, also
known as Shri Gusainji, continued his father's work and
greatly embellished the Path of Grace. In Adel Shri
Mahaprabhuji composed works that shed light upon the
loving path of devotion as well as the inner meanings of the
Upanishads, Bhagavat Gita, Brahma Sutra and the Shrimad
Bhagavatam.

When his devoted scribe Kashmiri Bhatt suddenly
died, Shri Vallabhacharya stopped his writing. He had
already heard Shri Krishna's second call to return to Him at
Madhuvan, in Vraj. Now, at the age of fifty-two, he informed
his wife that he was taking sannyasa and would renounce
his home and family.

Madhavendrapuri initiated Shri Vallabhacharya as a
sannyasi, and after remaining in his house in solitude for one
week, singing *Gopi Gita*, the Song of the Gopis, with tears
pouring from his eyes, he left his home and went to Benares,
where he spent another week alone on the banks of the holy
Ganga. Just before he returned to Shri Krishna's eternal Lila,
his family and disciples came before him, and the master
wrote his final teaching in the sands of the Ganga for them
to reflect upon:

If you in any way become turned away from Shri Krishna, your body, mind and everything that exists in the flow of time will most certainly be devoured. This is my conclusion. Shri Krishna is not worldly, nor does He accept any worldly worship performed by those who are turned away from Him. Our bhava for Him should be that Shri Krishna is our all and everything and will accomplish everything in this world or beyond. The Lord of the Gopis is to be worshipped with every devotional feeling and at all times.[20]

Then Shri Krishna suddenly appeared there by the Ganges and added,

If you believe in Me, the Beloved of the Gopis, then you are spiritually accomplished, and there is absolutely nothing else to be concerned with.[21]

In the year 1532 CE, Shri Mahaprabhu Vallabha-charya, Shri Krishna's very face, entered the Ganges River singing the verse,

Glories, Glories to You, Beloved Krishna. You have appeared in Vraj, where even Lakshmi takes Your constant shelter. With bated breath we search for You in all directions. O, Beloved! Come and look at us!

Then the Master's body ascended into the sky in a column of divine fire and merged into the Govardhan Hill hundreds of kilometers away. Shri Mahaprabhuji Vallabhacharya, the Beloved of Shri Krishna, entered into Shri Krishna's Lila with his physical form. He left us a rapturous path of devotion to contemplate and follow: "Always make Shri Krishna's seva." His son, Shri Vitthalnathji later wrote:

In this world you may find a great scholar, but will he understand the inner movement of the Vedas? Even if such a person exists, will his actions be consistent with his lofty precepts? You may be able to find such a person, but it is unlikely that he will be steeped in the loving path of Hari's worship. If you do find such a remarkable being, will he have loving devotion for Vrindavan Krishna, the Beloved of the Gopis? Besides Shri Vallabhacharya, no one is endowed with all of these qualities.

2.
SIDDHANT: THE TEACHINGS

INTRODUCTION

Siddhant is teaching that brings us to perfection. Siddhant is true philosophy. It is *siddha*, perfection, at the *anta* or end. Shri Vallabhacharya's siddhant is strictly for the attainment of Shri Krishna and is full of devotional, inspirational and practical advice for his followers. His words are replete with wisdom and love and are essential bhakti empowerments.

The Blessed Master's teachings nurture the delicate inner seed of devotion and guard it from the confusion and false identification that can cloud our vision and make us forget our true blissful nature. This seed of devotion begins as a subtle notion and can mature into a wishing tree that provides the blessed one with the priceless fruit of bhakti, the supreme unconditional devotion. In that blessed state, the Beloved appears in the heart and throughout creation, filling us with His own joy.

Between the 12th and 16th centuries, during the "bhakti renaissance," five great schools of Vaishnavism arose. They were founded by Shri Ramanuja, Shri Madhva, Shri Nimbarka, Shri Chaitanya and Shri Vallabhacharya. Shri Vallabhacharya's Path of Grace is followed today by tens of millions of people, mostly from North and West India. This school is unique in Vaishnavism for its philosophy of *Shuddhadvaita*, "pure non-dualism." Shri Vallabhacharya's shuddhadvaita affirms the existence of the world, holding it to be good, pure and joyful, indeed, not separate from the

Divine. This non-dualism is distinct from the teachings of Adi Shankara, which deny the world's true existence. With a devotional objective, let us now look at the siddhant, the teachings of Shri Vallabhacharya.

FIRST FIND THE RIGHT SOURCE

In spiritual life there must be not only a clear understanding of why a practice is undertaken, but also an intense desire to attain the desired object. It is always better to look toward the words of those who have had true insight into the sublime nature of Brahman rather than trying to independently formulate one's own conclusions. Shri Vallabhacharya tells us to absorb the teachings and wisdom of others who have come before us in divine realization.

Shri Vallabhacharya composed a remarkable body of spiritual teachings in Sanskrit based on the Vedas, Brahma Sutras, Upanishads, Bhagavat Gita, as well as the Shrimad Bhagavatam. His siddhant is referred to as *Brahmavada*, the reasoned doctrine that all is Brahman and nothing but Brahman. This pure non-dualist view supports the devotional view and practice of threading the mind into Shri Krishna.

CREATION

Shri Vallabhacharya is a pure monist and does not accept any duality between the soul, the world and Brahman. Brahman's bliss form is Krishna, Who is perfectly full of truth, consciousness and mostly joy. With the intention of expanding His own experience, in order to taste the joy of His own Being, Brahman manifested creation. The creation is simply another aspect of Brahman's formless, timeless, endless, full being. The Master of Speech, Shri Vallabhacharya explains that the world only appears as an illusion when vision is tainted with maya. When the confusion is removed, the world is seen as it is: made purely of Brahman.

Brahman stands at the beginning, middle and end of all things. He is existence, its cause, its support and end. He is the rays of the moon and the light of the sun. His forms are varied, and His face is hidden everywhere. Concealment and manifestation are Brahman's two powers whereby He brings forth this dance of creation. Shri Vallabhacharya's teachings inspire us to discover this Ultimate Reality within the world of beings.

The whole of creation is Shri Krishna's divine play. It is His Lila. We souls who have manifested into it are like sparks from a fire. We are His various actors appearing upon the authentic stage of this world. This inspiring view of oneness allows for diversity without dualistic animosity.

For Shri Vallabhacharya, philosophy is not merely intellectual, metaphysical, or a feat of refined logic. It endeavors to comprehend the nature of reality, for the aspirant must know the nature of Brahman before she can feel Him. When knowledge arises along with unconditional love, the soul joyfully experiences creation's blissful form. When it is celebrated within, there is an experience of all-encompassing love in the heart.

KRISHNA'S DIVINE NATURE

Shri Krishna is totally devoid of all material attributes, yet He is also personal and replete with divinity. Shri Krishna is able to respond to a wide variety of religious experiences. His multi-dimensional aspect was clearly demonstrated when He walked into Kamsa's wrestling stadium in Mathura. When He entered the arena, His parents looked upon Him as their son, while the women in the stands saw Him as Love Incarnate. The yogis observed Him as the absolute unblemished Brahman, while the cowherd lads saw Krishna as their friend. The wrestlers saw Him as a mighty foe, while King Kamsa viewed the divine cowlad as death personified. They all attained liberation due to their focus on Him, regardless of their personal view.

THE ILLUSIONS OF MAYA

Brahman's attributes appear in every object in the world. He is the clay as well as the various forms of clay-like pots and plates. Maya is simply a power of the Lord which is deluding and therefore creates false cognition. A person sees a white cloth as yellow when wearing yellow-tinted sunglasses. If one can discern that the white cloth is real and that the yellowness is a product of maya, then one can remove maya from one's perception without discarding the real world.

The Path of Grace sees everything as Krishna and nothing but Krishna. Since illusion, or maya, is a subject of perception, all objects in the world and the world itself are flawless. The pure non-dualist path embraces a positive and devotional worldview in which creation is seen as a perfect manifestation of Brahman. The blessed devotee is not obsessed with liberation or any other form of yoga besides the pleasing service to Shri Krishna.

DIVINITY IN THE WORLD

Those who realize Brahman perceive the world as Brahman's form, which is absolutely pure. Those who have knowledge but lack love view the world as a mixture of maya and Brahman. The ignorant ones cannot find Brahman anywhere.

Although all things are equally Brahman, for Shri Vallabhacharya, the Yamuna and Ganges Rivers, as well as sacred items, places and people are set apart from the rest of the world, for they have helped people realize Brahman. If one is confused and sees the body as the soul, it is a condition of false identification. At that moment Brahman is not recognized as the Self of all things; the individual has forgotten his or her true joyful nature.

THE UNCONTRIVED PATH

Devotees on the Path of Grace celebrated the nectar of Shri Krishna's presence with refined sensitivities. This path is the uncontrived spiritual route, and Shri Vallabhacharya has taught that the means and the reward should be seen as one. Each level of realization is a part of the divine Lila, and Shri Krishna is the Master of ceremonies. Therefore, the result is always perfect.

THE SOUL

The Taittriya Upanishad reveals that when Brahman desired to play, though He was One, He became many. In the Gita Shri Krishna proclaims, "In the world of beings, souls are My very parts." A soul is either pure, bound or liberated. Before the soul manifests into the world, it is a pure part of God. At the time it appears in this world of matter, however, most souls become bound, and their bliss is concealed. When souls are able to remove their false identifications with their body, senses, life-force, and faculty of cognition, they are able to become re-established with Brahman, and they become blissful again.

Souls can achieve liberation while in the body or after death. Blessed souls are divine in nature and perform Shri Krishna's loving seva. Souls who follow the laws of scriptures are eligible for liberation, while mundane souls receive worldly rewards.[22]

The soul is atomic in nature and pervasive in effect, just as a small amount of sandalwood paste cools the entire body when applied merely to the forehead. The soul lives in the heart, and as the Brahma Sutra states, "permeates consciousness throughout the body."

The five knots of ignorance keep the soul in bondage, as Shri Vallabhacharya describes in his *Shastrarth Prakarana*: "The five knots of ignorance are the body, senses, life-force, inner cognitive faculties as well as your spiritual being, when they are not recognized as being connected to God."

When the soul becomes liberated, either through wisdom or devotion, it no longer revolves in the karmic wheel and is free from rebirth. Liberation can occur while living in the body, or it can be attained after leaving the body. Grace filled souls enter into Shri Krishna's eternal Lila. The law-abiding souls merge with Brahman, while worldly souls continue to take birth here in the world.

THE BHAKTAS' DISPOSITION

Some bhaktas are pure in nature *(sattvik)*, some are passionate *(rajas)*, while others are obstinate *(tamas)*. Bhaktas of every disposition are accepted by Shri Krishna. Once all virtues are directed towards Him, every emotion can be useful in His worship. The bhaktas' dispositions are but various devotional fuels that propel them towards the Lord. Since it is too difficult to transcend this world of matter, Shri

Krishna appears here and plays with the soul according to her nature.

TRANSFORMING DEVOTION

First, there arises the subtle and blessed understanding that Shri Krishna is Brahman and deserves ultimate adoration. Then, a desire for a specific relationship with Him arises. This is followed by practice, and when Shri Krishna responds, the fruit is attained.

The practice of devotion to Shri Krishna is transforming. Like gutter water that spills into Ganga becomes Ganga, similarly, in the Path of Grace, anything offered to Shri Krishna becomes like Him, free of bondage. In the devotional process, everything leads to the Blessed Lord.

BOUND ONLY BY LOVE

On the subject of practice, Shri Vallabhacharya is concise: "The attainment of Shri Krishna can never be dependent upon any formula. Shri Krishna, who is perfect bhava, is attained through the precise emulation of those who have already attained Him."[23] As the Gopis of Vrindavan are the ones who attained Krishna, they are the gurus of the grace filled Path.

If God could be captured by a particular formula, that prisoner could not be God. After Krishna stole the butter, His mother, Yashoda could only tie Him up after He allowed her to. Although Brahman cannot be confined, Shri Krishna allows Himself to be bound by the devotees' cords of love.

SHRI KRISHNA

The primordial nature is Shri Krishna. He is the Supreme Being. Etymologically, *krish* means "being" and *na* means "bliss." Krishna is the all-attractive One. He tells Arjuna in the Gita, "O Arjuna, nothing is superior to Me....I am even greater than that impersonal form of Brahman."

Shri Vallabhacharya says, "The Supreme Brahman is Krishna alone."[24] Krishna is devoid of mundane limbs, hands and feet. The *Svetasvatara Upanishad* states, "He runs quickly and grabs without hands and feet....His hands, feet, face, stomach etc. all embody bliss."

Shri Krishna is the Supreme Person and eternally manifests all divine qualities. Krishna is also *ras* (pure nectar) and can respond to the loving devotion of His bhaktas. Krishna is a divine dancer, player, actor, husband, cowherder, friend, Lover, as well as a flute player. He is an expert in *abhinaya* – that is, in exhibiting the meaning of what He depicts. He is so good that anyone who has contact with Him or His lila-drama has an unforgettable experience. Love, attachment and obsession are the results.

Shri Krishna and His worship are pure divine drama (Lila). He plays and directs at the same time, all for an awakening in those whose time has come. His bhaktas have various constitutions, yet share the common virtue of Krishna attachment. Their hearts are fired by His melody and contain the rush of His *ras*. It is all consummated in Vrindavan, where Krishna plays His flute.

It is Shri Krishna's sheer confidence that allows Him to establish overwhelming attachment to Himself in whomever He chooses. In Vrindavan everything is a combination of Him. Even trees and animals fall under His spell and become enlightened. In Vrindavan everything manifests for the blissful purpose of Lila. Krishna sounds His flute to awaken the woods. Krishna is proficient in appearing and appealing to the bhakta according to her individual temperament. Shri Krishna comes here and manifests sacred creation. Lila makes Krishna comprehensible.

CHILD KRISHNA – ADOLESCENT KRISHNA

To most people it appears that Krishna is an innocent Child. Mother Yashodaji, Sri Nandarayaji, Rohiniji, and other elderly cowherd folk regard Him purely as a child and are not privy to His other lilas. His intimate Vraja devotees, the Gopis, know that He is most adept in all lilas. When they are before Yashoda, they cleverly act as if they know nothing, but actually, they know Shri Krishna's loving side very well. They become shy whenever they see His form, which is so filled with effulgence and beauty that millions of love-gods are humbled to see it.[25] Shri Krishna gives the experience of all lilas simultaneously. Shri Krishna is truly a divine Child and perfectly contains all contradictions. Shri Gusainji has written in his cradle song,

> As Infant Krishna swings in the cradle,
> He eliminates Radha's annoyance in love.

SHRI KRISHNA,
THE BHAKTAS' FAMILY MEMBER

Shri Vallabhacharya stressed that devotional practice should be done in the home, which is why the Path of Grace has remained almost entirely a householder lineage. It is the devotee's duty to honor Shri Krishna as the Lord of Gokul, the Supreme Brahman and also as a member of one's household. One must always serve Him with bhava, the unconditional loving attitude. Devotion is perfected by offering one's body, wealth and mind-heart to the Blessed Lord. In this state of dedication, true renunciation develops.

BRAHMAN'S DIFFERENT FORMS

The Supreme can appear either as Shri Krishna, the impersonal Brahman or as the foundation of Brahman's abode. Bhaktas see this world and the formless Brahman as the foundation of His Lila. Followers of the path of knowledge see Brahman as truth, consciousness and bliss, transcending time, and place. Brahman is self-illuminating and beyond all material qualities.

The Lord also exists as the inner controller (*antaryami*) who controls all things from within, as well as the divinities which preside over the sun, earth and other heavenly bodies. The Brahdaranyaka Upanishad says, "Whoever governs this and other worlds as well as all creatures from within is the inner controller." All incarnations appear from this inner controller and are partial manifestations of Shri Krishna.

GRACE

Shri Krishna's grace is the soul's nourishment. Shri Vallabhacharya explains, "Pushti is Krishna's grace. It nullifies the influence of time, action and nature." Grace can provide either mundane or divine fruit. Shri Vallabhacharya adds here, "Grace is a divine secret, yet it is proven because its effects are seen in the world."

Grace refers to that which removes powerful obstacles and provides the realization of God's feet. The Shrimad Bhagavat explains, "As the Ganges flows incessantly towards the ocean, similarly, our minds should flow constantly towards the Lord." When we are pulled towards the ocean of Krishna awareness, it is a condition of grace.

Devotion that arises from grace is called Blessed Devotion, in which there is no desire for any reward other than the sincere wish to acquire the Lord as the fruit of life. The Bhagavat states, "Lovely Krishna alone is the reward for all those who possess eyes."

Shri Vallabhacharya writes in his treatise, *Tattvarthdeep Nibandha*, "When the soul relies upon Krishna, it is a rule of law, but when the Lord relies upon the soul, it is an exception of grace."

The Bhagavat relates, "The residents of Vrindavan toiled all day long tending to their cows and performing other pastoral chores. Exhausted from their day of work, they slept soundly throughout the night. Yet, Shri Krishna allowed them entrance into His divine abode." Their attainment was effortless, and so this is yet another example of grace.

BHAVA

The Path of Grace is a fiery affair. Shri Krishna is known through grace but responds to devout intensity. There must be mutual attraction. The Blessed Lord dances according to the nature of his inspired bhaktas. He is bound by the cords of their love. The divine exchange often arises with the guru's intervention. He performs the marriage ceremony between the soul and Brahman.

Bhaktas are distinguished by their *bhava* (their enlightened emotional perception). It is the realization of Brahman coupled with overwhelming love. Bhava touches essence. When oblivion is obliterated, with bhava, the devotional spark becomes ablaze and consumes the soul's binding karmas.

THE BLESSED PATH

Shri Harirayaji, Shri Vallabhacharya's great, great grandson, was a very important teacher in the history of the Path of Grace. His explanations of the Path of Grace are concise:

"When the absence of all means is the means to achieve the fruit, and when the fruit is the means, know that to be the Blessed Path.

"When worldly and scriptural achievements are accomplished through the Lord's grace alone and never through the devotee's efforts, know this to be the Blessed Path.

"When the Lord accepts the soul without considering her qualifications and does so without delay, know this to be the Blessed Path.

"When a devotee who has understood the intention of the scriptural injunctions remains attached to the Lord Himself and has no obsession for scriptural practice, know this to be the Blessed Path.

"When there is no consideration of virtue or defect, and when there is a continual feeling of appreciation for all the Lord's deeds, know this to be the Blessed Path.

"When thought is never given to worldly and scriptural satisfaction, but only to pleasing the Lord, know this to be the Blessed Path.

"When there is not an infinitesimal reason for the Lord's selection of the soul and the choice depends solely upon His divine sweet will, know this to be the Blessed Path.

"When devotion is independent, does not require the external manifestation of the Lord, and leads to all types of divine experiences, know this to be the Blessed Path.

"When there is no fear of the world and the scriptures because of profuse divine attachment, and when everything other than the Blessed Lord appears as an obstacle, know this to be the Blessed Path.

"When relationship is both the means and the achievement and is established according to Krishna's sweet desire, know this to be the Blessed Path.

"When anything related to the Lord is treated as if it is the Lord Himself, anything unrelated is treated with indifference, and anything in opposition to the Lord is opposed, know this to be the Blessed Path.

"When no concern is shown for one's body, etc. and a keen desire for Him always lingers, know this to be the Blessed Path.

"When devotion has no expectation for reciprocation, and when the divine sentiment is nourished, know this to be the Blessed Path.

"When the Lord in no case provides the devotee with the fruit of worship because the ripening of his divine attachment requires that the fruit be withheld, know this to be the Blessed Path.

"When one is happier in the Lord's separation than in His union because of the inner experience of all His lilas, know this to be the Blessed Path.

"When there is a reversal in the order of the means and attainment, and when devotional attachment is the attainment as well as the means, know this to be the Blessed Path.

"When there is a constant feeling of divine melancholy concerning all of His activities and the bhakta's excessive eagerness to experience the Lord's lilas produces humility, know this to be the Blessed Path.

"When humility is the singular means for the Lord's manifestation, and the humility aroused in separation is the fruit, know this to be the Blessed Path.

"When there is renunciation of all sensual objects and dedication of the body, etc. with bhava for the Lord, know this to be the Blessed Path.

"When the soul always feels remembered by Krishna due to total attachment to His feet and is able to forget mundane pleasures, that is the Blessed Path.

"Keeping Shri Vallabhacharya in our hearts, one should always understand and rely specifically on the Blessed Path in the above-mentioned way."

ELIGIBILITY

One becomes eligible for and inclined towards the Blessed Path by the Lord's grace. It is through the blessed Lord's grace that souls have association with His bhaktas. The Shrimad Bhagavat states, "By always serving holy souls, my mind was purified, and I became sincerely inclined towards the divine practice."

Shri Vallabhacharya says, "In all transcendental matters, inclination comes from hearing about Shri Krishna's greatness." When there is an inner experience of the Lord, then the seed of divine mood grows, along with a distinct and conscious inclination, by means of devotional listening and other bhakti practices. It sprouts into the form of love and removes attachment to everything except the Lord. Then follows the divine state of attachment and in the ultimate condition, the bhakta becomes addicted to Shri Krishna.

"Devotees who have direct devotion without motive for the Supreme Person do not leave My worship to accept anything, even the four types of liberation" (Shrimad Bhagavat). This type of devotion is referred to as intense bhakti yoga, and it arises from profound love for God.

TOTAL LOVE

Total love (*sarvatma-bhava*) is an advanced stage of devotion characterized by unconditional love for the Lord. The word 'bhava' here means love, for it is said, "Love for the Lord and other divine things is called bhava."

The love within the soul is called *atmabhava*, as in: "We love our children not for their own sake, but for the sake of our own soul" (Brahadaranyaka 2.4.51). As one loves oneself, similarly, there should be love for the Lord. Then there is a unity between the Supreme and the soul. In the Path of Grace, love of the Lord is not based on duality, but occurs because the Self naturally possesses a feeling of unity. Kamsa always viewed Krishna with hostility and was awarded liberation because of his focus on Him. Just imagine the divine condition of those who love Him!

Total love is to have a feeling of identity between the Lord and all things. Lawful love and grace filled love are the two types of total love. Lawful love makes one feel God's presence in all things. In grace filled love, like that experienced by the Gopis in their separation from Krishna, one experiences Him everywhere. This love is greater than the total love in the Path of Law because of the many amorous sentiments for the Lord included in that total love. These and other devotional moods are very useful in experiencing the great joy of devotion.

THE REWARD OF DEVOTION

When a bhakta becomes possessed by Krishna, the Blessed Lord's presence is experienced in the world as He sports with His unimaginable powers. *Nirodha* is when the Blessed Lord possesses His beloved ones according to their individual nature. Through His different types of lilas, He makes His bhaktas forget the world and creates an everlasting link with them. Shri Vallabhacharya remarks, "Those whom Hari has liberated from Himself are absorbed into the worldly ocean, while those whom He binds to Himself surely experience supreme joy day and night."[26]

A person absorbed in the mayic world is not qualified for nirodha. Attachment to Shri Krishna allows the bhakta divine entrance. This transforms the bhakta and makes her unattached to anything that is unrelated to Him. The bhakta's reality is described in the Shrimad Bhagavat: "While sleeping, eating, wandering around, speaking, playing, bathing and sitting and moving about, the residents of Vrindavan were unaware of themselves. They were completely engrossed in Krishna."

LILA

The divine Lila that the Lord performs is always increasing in bliss. The realization of Krishna's Lila is the devotional dharma of the soul. Shri Vallabhacharya says, "The Lord's birth occurs when Hari incarnates in the world, with all powers of action, in order to bless everyone with His sight. Those bhaktas who adhere their minds to Him forget the false world and become divinely attached" (Bhagavatartha 10.20).

THE GOPIS' DEVOTON

The bhaktas of Vraj cherished obstinate love for Shri Krishna and were devoid of any knowledge unrelated to His lilas. They transgressed the rules of the world and Vedas, because they were only interested in Krishna. Shri Krishna praises them, "They have left the world, the Vedas and their relatives for Me."

The Gopis of Vrindavan are the gurus of the Path of Grace. The way they serve and love Shri Krishna is the highest example of devotion, and Shri Vallabhacharya teaches that their devotion should be emulated. Their lives were full of Krishna, and they found Him everywhere. To attain Gopihood is the height of devotion. Shri Gusainji has provided us with a beautiful description of the Gopis' bhava:

"I adore the divine Vrindavan wishing tree which grants the deer-eyed Gopis total love for Shri Krishna. At first, the Gopis' bhava for Krishna is a sprout that has been nourished for a very long time. When their love becomes firm, it becomes a sapling. When longing to be with Krishna increases, their devotional saplings grow hundreds of branches. When Shri Krishna fulfills the Gopis' divine desires by interacting with them in numerous ways, their devotional branches fill out with lovely leaves. The joy that arises from their exchanges with Shri Krishna blossoms, and when their desire to join Him increases even more, those blossoms become flowers. Finally, when Shri Krishna engages with them according to their bhava and fulfills their every desire, the blessed wishing tree becomes laden with fruit."

PLEASING SHRI KRISHNA

A follower of Shri Vallabhacharya once explained to another bhakta how to know when Shri Krishna is pleased with a bhakta's seva: "There are four indications. First, devotees naturally go to homes where seva is made. The second indication is that Shri Nathji's form fills their hearts with bliss as they reflect, 'Through the grace of Shri Mahaprabhu Vallabhacharya and Shri Gusainji, Shri Krishna comes and accepts my water and cooking.'

"The third sign is that just as they adorn Shri Krishna, so He appears. The fourth indication is that the offerings made to Shri Krishna in Shri Mahaprabhuji's name have many different divine tastes, and the plate of prasad does not diminish. When all this occurs, know that Shri Krishna is pleased with the bhakta's seva."

That bhakta went to another follower's house and asked, "How can we please Shri Krishna?" The second bhakta explained, "Shri Krishna is pleased with the ones whom Shri Swaminiji (Shri Radha) is pleased with. Then She showers Her blessings. Know that Shri Swaminiji is pleased when the bhakta's faith becomes firm and they have one-pointed devotion to Shri Mahaprabhuji, Shri Gusainji, Shri Nathji, as well as to Shri Swaminiji and all Their bhaktas. Then know that Shri Krishna has blessed the bhakta. This path is solely Shri Swaminiji's. When She is pleased, Shri Krishna allows the soul entrance into the Lila. When that happens, know that Shri Krishna is delighted."

Then the bhakta went to Krishna Bhatt and said, "I want to know how to please Shri Krishna."

Krishna Bhatt replied, "Know that Shri Krishna and Shri Swaminiji are so absorbed in Their own bliss that Their attention does not wander elsewhere. They are perfectly enchanted with Their own Lila and lost in each other's forms. There is one intimate sakhi who always remains nearby. When she is pleased with someone, she sings that bhakta's glories to the Divine Couple. This pleases them, and then they fulfill that bhakta's wishes.

"There is yet another Gopi who cares for all the outer arrangements in the Lila. She is an attendant of the lila-bower and arranges the bed and ornaments. She stands by the door of the lila-bower and sings very sweetly. She praises the Divine Couple in various ways. Sometimes she makes divine requests on behalf of certain individuals to Shri Swaminiji's intimate Gopi at just the right time. In turn, that

Gopi keeps it in her heart, and when Shri Krishna and Shri Swaminiji are in a celebratory mood, she reminds them of that bhakta. Then Shri Krishna becomes pleased with that bhakta.

"Just as a woman who desires a man can arrange the meeting through her female messenger, similarly, in the path of loving devotion, the bhakta who knows the Lord is the messenger for other bhaktas. Know that Shri Krishna is found when we please such a bhakta."

LILA CONTEMPLATION

"After offering Shri Krishna lunch, devotional contemplation should be done. Quietly reflect how Shri Krishna takes His meals at home during the winter season. Follow Krishna when He is invited to the Gopi's house. During the hot season, contemplate Shri Krishna's lunch in the forest by the banks of the Yamuna, in the forest at Shyamdak, or other places where He grazes His cows and plays with His cowlad friends. When Shri Krishna is hungry, see how He climbs a tree to look for the Gopis who are bringing His lunch. Sometimes when the Gopis lose their way, Krishna sounds His flute to show them the path. Feel the groups of Gopis coming from their homes with lunch baskets balanced on their heads. Shri Krishna enjoys their offerings and gives the leftovers to His friends. Krishna plays in so many ways.

Sometimes He grabs the food, laughs and then gives the Gopis secret messages about an evening rendezvous. There are so many bhavas to contemplate. During the rainy season, Radha and Krishna come to the Vrindavan forest, which is delightful to behold. Dark clouds fill the sky, and when Shri Swaminiji gets wet from the rain, Shri Krishna dries her with the edge of His blanket. Shri Krishna enchants

Radha and takes her to bowers filled with precious jewels. She implores Krishna, 'You enjoy the offerings first.' They exchange sweet words while Lalita and other Gopis serve the Divine Couple and enjoy the lila. Know that Shri Krishna responds directly to the bhava of His pure bhakta" (252 *Vaishnavas, Part One,* varta #52).

PRESENT DAY SOULS

Shri Krishna told Uddhava, "By following dharma and surrendering one's soul to Me, devotion is received." To give the special reward, the Blessed Lord plants the seed of devotion within those who belong to the Path of Grace.

Present day bhaktas learn about obstructions to devotional life from the guru's teachings. By performing Shri Krishna's worship, ignorance can be removed. When Shri Krishna incarnated and slew the demoness Putana, He removed the ignorance from His bhaktas' hearts. Present day bhaktas need to seek Hari's shelter to remove their ignorance, and they should avoid all impure association. After hearing the divine names from other blessed bhaktas, they should remember the sacred names' precise form, attributes and lila connections while repeating them. Then without them even knowing it, the Lord removes numerous obstructions.

Just as mother Yashoda remembered and sang about Shri Krishna's lilas as she churned the curds, present day bhaktas should sing Shri Krishna's praises while engaged in worldly tasks. Senses that are turned away from God can become purified through devotional practices and then adhered to the Lord. Know that Bhakti yoga has been highly praised because those who practice it can overcome the three material qualities and achieve perfect love for the Lord. The sacred Shruti texts have also advised transcendental enjoyment with the Supreme Being.

THE GRACE FILLED REWARD

"The reward of Shri Vallabh's path has manifested for those who have flawless devotion. The scriptural type of devotional practice can also be followed, but the experience of the highest reward is found in the devotion of the Gopis of Vrindavan. They have beautiful eyes and dance with Krishna right in their homes! In the Path of Grace, whatever, whenever and in whatever way the bhaktas offer Shri Krishna something He desires, He appears to them directly as the Lord of the Gopis. Then His lotus face laughs as He affectionately accepts the offerings."

– Shri Gusainji

3.
SHRI SUBODHINI

These Shri Subodhini passages are Shri Vallabhacharya's teachings on the *Venu Gita* – Song of the Flute, found in the tenth canto of the Shrimad Bhagavatam. Shri Subodhini contains the essence of the Master's devotional heart and gives, as its name implies, beautiful intelligence. Shri Subodhini is a refined blend of exalted Vedantic teaching infused with the bhava of the Vrindavan Gopis.

KRISHNA AWAKENS

Before there is attachment, however, love must arise, and only Hari can cause this awakening....Lila is replete with purpose, and Krishna awakens only those whose time has come. Others simply will not respond to His calling.

KRISHNA IS THE LORD OF SPRING

Krishna is the Lord of spring, the supreme season of love. Hari is comprised of nectar. His bhava supports the conjugal exchange.

THE GREATEST REWARD

The Swaminis know of no greater reward for those endowed with eyes than to behold Krishna and Balaram playing their flutes and herding cows.

LILA NECTAR

Divine nectar is independent. It is not tasted by practice, but arrives on its own accord. It is concealed. It resides and develops in the realms of utmost secrecy. When overly revealed, improperly displayed, or unguarded, it vanishes. To protect this delicate devotional elixir, Krishna wears cloth as brilliant as gold. It baffles and bedazzles.

VEILED GLORY

What is profound cannot be inappropriately displayed. For this reason Hari uses maya to veil His own glory. If His *pitambar*, His golden shawl, is so radiant that it is impossible to gaze at, then what to speak of the nectar ras that surges behind it in the very form of Shri Krishna!

KRISHNA LIKES THE SUBLIME

Krishna only likes what is sublime and delightful. It is only when nectar completely engulfs the soul that the blessed one can come face to face with Hari. This is a divine state of consciousness wherein the bhakta becomes oblivious to the world.

REVERSED ROLES

First Krishna enjoyed the Gopis, and then Krishna was enjoyed by them. The roles became reversed in the surge of grace. The Swaminis enjoyed Krishna the way He enjoyed them.

LOTUS FEET

Krishna's lotus feet are the very form of devotion. They purify. They have appeared not only for play, but to establish bhakti in Hari's people.

SECRET TEACHING

Krishna's essence is His love. His bhava for Swamini is the true meaning of blissful Krishna. It is also the secret essential teaching of the Blessed Path.

THE FLUTE'S CALL

The call of Hari's flute is enchanting to all, regardless of position or aptitude. It is all-attractive, like Krishna Himself.

BLISS PENETRATED

The Gopis sang and rejoiced. They were oblivious to all the pains of the world. They dallied in the ocean of Supreme Bliss, no longer obstructed by overwhelming desires that blocked their bhakti-filled hearts. Hari's nectar made its way into their souls and completely penetrated their beings.

BHAKTI'S GREATNESS

When the unconscious becomes conscious, and when rivers stop their flow to listen, the greatness of bhakti is revealed.

SUPREME REWARD

"To behold Him with eyes, or better yet with all senses, and to imbibe His form, His divine essence, is the only reward for us." For those who know how to employ their senses in Shri Krishna's pleasure, liberation appears as pure bondage. You must leave behind only one thing: anything which is not for His pleasure. The reward for those who experience Shri Krishna's Bliss within and without and through all channels of perception stands far above those who know Him merely as impersonal Brahman, devoid of all attire.

ONE-POINTED LOVE

"Our love is one-pointed. We see the Beloved's face everywhere. All forms have become His expansions. Our love for Hari is complete."

RAS

Only when *ras* (nectar) appears can it be tasted. Once it is tasted, there is dance and beauty. In Lila, Krishna reveals esoteric ras. Know it to be the supreme secret arising in the company of the Vrindavan Swaminis.

DIVINE ITEMS

Divine items are always filled with consciousness, regardless of what they are or where they live.

UNCOMMON EXPERIENCE

To be totally full of bliss and to have your hairs stand on end are not common experience, yet, in Vrindavan, even trees and rivers experience that.

INDEPENDENT KRISHNA

Krishna is independent and only reveals Himself occasionally. Not even Vrindavan has the power to bring forth His darshan. Only by means of devotion is His vision attained everywhere. Without devotion, however, even Vrindavan becomes devoid of fame.

UNCONDITIONAL LORDSHIP

Whenever you see the simple-minded worship the Blessed Lord unpromptedly, know that Unconditional Lordship has appeared within the world of beings.

REFUGE

When you transcend your lower nature, you attain true knowledge. Then there is refuge and dedication, which creates love for Hari's lotus feet.

TWO WISDOMS

Bhagavat gyan (knowledge of Hari) is to know what Shri Krishna needs at any time or place. *Sva gyan* (knowledge of Self) is knowing how to offer magnificent things to Him. When we do not know when, where, how or what types of items to offer Hari, the undertaking becomes fruitless. Know how to connect everything to Hari. Know what He likes. By knowing these two wisdoms (knowledge of Hari and Self), worship becomes refined and meaningful.

BLISSFUL SIGHT

The sight of Krishna is blissful, and Krishna sadhana is joyous. Blessed is the bhava of His attachment. It provides constant elation.

THE ULTIMATE NECTAR

The conjugal mood is described in holy lore as the ultimate ras. It is the exalted state, the only true mood. It is the substratum of the true drama, and without it, there is simply no taste. For this reason it is held in the highest esteem. As gold is the best metal to adorn the Great One, similarly the amorous mood is the supreme mood. All other nectars are contained within its dimensions, and without it, knowers of ras could never take delight.

THE BIRDS

The Vrindavan birds are seers – contemplative and patient. They are watching and waiting for Shri Krishna to walk through their forest. They wait for their great opportunity in the protective arms of the noble Vrindavan woods, which are also considered to be high incarnations. From their elevated branches, the winged ones will behold Hari only after relishing the call of His flute.

THE WATERS

It is the natural dharma for rivers and springs to flow, but in Vrindavan things are very different. The profound desires of the waters' hearts are filled with wisdom and discrimination. Those springs and rivers now stop their flow, not due to weakness or formula, but only to meet with Hari.

THE CLOUD

One who is born and can develop and cultivate devotion to the Lord attains *atmanivedanam*. One cloud perfected this blessed state of soulful dedication. Some compare that cloud to Krishna, since she is charitable like Hari. She also shares His hue and like Him, nourishes and helps create life with her life-giving waters. Those who share similar qualities are generally friends. This cloud excels even in friendship. She has given everything she owns to Krishna. She freely offers her nectar essence of flowers to Hari in an act of selfless love.

THE GOVARDHAN HILL

The Govardhan Hill is pure and *nirguna* – devoid of worldly virtues and filled with divine qualities. Although penniless, the Hill offers water, grass, caves and roots to the cows, the cowlads, gods, as well as Ram and Krishna. The Govardhan Hill is a fine host to its divine guests. Four items necessary for good hospitality are always found in the saint's abode: a grass mat to sit on, a place on the earth to entertain, water to refresh the guest, and sweet speech that is pleasing to the mind.

The following Shri Subodhini passages are from the *Chir Haran* Lila chapter in which Shri Krishna stole the Gopis' clothes, only to later award them divine garments which transformed their very beings.

DHARMA FORTUNE

A person who has a doubt concerning the nature of dharma should look to one who is grounded in it. Only blessed beings receive the fruit of dharma. When dharma is absent, barriers arise. The fortune of true dharma is immense. The person who understands the "dharma fortune" attains fame and is appreciated by all.

SERVICE TO OTHERS

Life and dharma become exquisite when they are employed in the service of others. Activities done with selfish motives are always inferior. Mediocrity reigns when actions mingle with selfish and selfless motives. The highest course of action is exemplified by Rantideva. While he himself fasted, he gave food to others. His deeds are grounds for liberation.

THE VRINDAVAN TREES

The trees of Vrindavan are most blessed and support all of life. Their existence is fruitful because they advance the lives of others. This honorable nature is seen in saints. Like trees, saints never turn away anyone who desires something which they can provide....When a tree dies, its branches no longer obstruct the bird's view, and its body can be cut and used as fuel. Even after dying, the tree, like a great renunciate, is always beyond the snares of death.

THE TREE'S OPEN HOME

The home of a tree is its shade, which is available to all. Human homeowners do not invite everyone inside, and their guests can also create conflict.

THE TREE'S SERVICE

Trees serve and protect us from excessive heat, cold and rain. Dharma is found in the roots of trees, which provide medicinal herbs.... From the tree's wood and bark, garments and vessels are made. Even the tree's dead branches are useful, unlike the brittle bodies of humans which can no longer be enjoyed after death. The fragrance of trees constitutes their fame. The fame of a man or his name does not serve us at all. The inner essence of trees is their resin. It is their speech. Even ash from the burned tree is useful in washing things. The ashes from human cremations are useless and considered impure. When the dead body becomes a ghost, purification rites have to be performed for the ultimate release of the deceased. The partially burned portions of a tree become coal, an excellent heating source, while the charred remains of a dead body should not even be touched. Finally, the small branches of a tree are like good servants. Trees fulfill the wishes of all people.

ACCOMPLISHED BEINGS

Birth is productive when there are no obstructing selfish concerns. Enlightened beings see all things, even their children and family, as arising through the wish of Hari. Accomplished ones do not feel as though they are the doers in any situation.

FOR THE BENEFIT OF OTHERS

The blessed ones who understand that Bhagavan has created everything for everyone use all they have for the benefit of others. They are like God; they are equal to an avatar. Their births are fruitful.

TOTAL OFFERING

Krishna's form of wisdom outshines a billion suns. Every mind and heart is under His hold. When the mind is offered to Him, everything associated with that being becomes dedicated. This total offering is revealed when Shri Krishna tells the Gopis that they are "absorbed into Me." They are not only dedicated, but they are enthralled and totally established.

HIS PERSONAL TOUCH

Shri Krishna knows that the Gopis did not come to Him for worldly marriage or sensual enjoyment. They do not contradict the ways of the world, nor do they desire wisdom. Those blessed girls contemplated the situation from every angle and arrived there only for love. They confirm this by longing to touch His feet. Through bhakti yoga, they only desired Krishna. They crave His devotional touch and now have no interest in even hearing about Him. There is no longer any desire to practice anything else, not even the devotion of being His friend. All they want is His personal contact. It is not merely a longing, but a clear desire to employ their bodies and senses in the sacred act.

ACTION AND KNOWLEDGE

After telling the Gopis to emerge from the river with their hands above their heads, Shri Krishna explains, "Gopis, this act of folding your hands will permeate everything with knowledge. It occurs when your power of action contained in the folding of your hands is raised towards your head, the seat of knowledge. This protects your Self from the worldly flow and establishes you firmly with Me. Then wisdom arises everywhere, and the Lord is pleased. Knowers of sacred lore tell us that the reward is attained when actions mature and converge with knowledge. Then there is true accomplishment."

BHAKTI DHARMA

Good association with accomplished devotees grants the attainment of Shri Krishna. Similarly, when the Gopis' garments had the association of the Kadamba tree, a great bhakta, they became filled with devotional dharma.

THE GOPIS' VIRTUES

The virtues which appear in the various Gopis are all examples for us to understand the nature of divine attributes. The Gopis of Vrindavan are not part of the worldly creation. They appear only for the sake of Lila. They are various bhava forms which appear in response to Shri Krishna, the embodiment of the unshakeable nectar. Know that Shri Krishna's Lila creation is eternal and totally divine. It is not part of the world that Brahma creates; it is purely Shri Krishna's.

HIS MERE PRESENCE

Since Shri Krishna is the Lord of the lord of yogis, He is able to remove imperfections from within others. A single lord of yogis, through his power of Yoga, is able to enter a being and cleanse that soul of impurities wherever he or she may reside. Shri Krishna is the Lord of even those lords of yogis, and so He does not even have to enter them to remove their shortcomings. Everything is accomplished through His mere presence.

KRISHNA ONLY KNOWS HIS BHAKTAS

Shri Krishna is all-knowing, but when He engages in the grace filled cause, He is only aware of His bhaktas. Shri Krishna perfectly supports all contradictions. The stealing of the Gopis' garments is a part of His grace filled Lila. There is no fault here. Krishna does not contradict any lawful course, and this play of His contains supreme merit.

4.
SHRI VITTHALNATHJI
(SHRI GUSAINJI)

When Shri Vallabhacharya visited Vitthalnathji's temple in Pandarpur, the Blessed Lord personally told him to marry so that He could appear as his son. When his second son was born, the master recognized him as the Lord's manifestation and named him Shri Vitthalnathji. He later became known as Shri Gusainji. Shri Vitthalnathji was born in 1516 in Charanat, a village near Benares. He was a playful child and had keen interest in the stories of Shri Krishna's childhood. Shri Vitthalnathji was first under his father's guidance and later received further inspiration from his father's main disciple, Damodardas Harsani.

Shri Gusainji became the head of the Pushti lineage after the early passing of his elder brother, Shri Gopinathji. A master of the non-dual bhakti tradition, Shri Gusainji composed approximately fifty devotional texts, including commentaries on his father's writings. His contributions to the grace filled lineage are as important as Shri Vallabhacharya's own. His teachings provide insights necessary to understand the inner mood of the lineage. Shri Gusainji's Sanskrit poems are the only songs which are daily sung in Shri Krishna's seva.

Shri Gusainji lived during the Mughal occupation in north India. Hindu temples were being destroyed, and Vedic dharma was under attack. During this dark period, Shri Gusainji was able to promote the Path of Grace and infuse it with grandeur. Only an Acharya of his divine stature could create a devotional renaissance amidst times of turmoil.

Shri Gusainji filled the Path of Grace with profound Lila bhava. He was not only a protector of dharma, but also a poet, musician, artist, and profound bhakti teacher. He elaborated Shri Krishna's divine worship with music, exquisite food offerings, ornamentation and other arts. He taught that only things of the highest quality should be offered to Shri Krishna, the Lord of refined enjoyments. He showed the world how to worship Shri Krishna with opulence and grace. His seva teachings became the very heart of the Path of Grace, and the modes of seva observed today in temples like Shri Nathji's, as well as in the homes of his followers, are the result of his genius. His inspiration flowed into every aspect of the grace filled worship.

Shri Gusainji fulfilled the wishes not only of his disciples, but of Shri Krishna as well. His aesthetic sensibilities were rich with devotion and filled the Path of Grace with Shri Krishna's presence. During these times, Shri Krishna spoke and played directly with Shri Gusainji and his disciples. Shri Gusainji is the master of devotion.

The Mughal Emperor of India, Akbar had deep respect for Shri Gusainji and issued a number of Shahi Farmans (imperial proclamations) to him as marks of special favor. Courtiers and noblemen including Birbal, Raja Todarmal, Tansen, and Baz Bahadur became devoted to Shri Gusainji. Akbar also commissioned special paintings of Shri Nathji, Shri Navnit Priyaji as well as of Shri Vitthalnathji and his seven sons.

Emperor Akbar often came to visit Shri Gusainji and was allowed to see Shri Krishna's seva. He gifted Shri Nathji an enormous diamond which still today rests on the Blessed Lord's chin. A well known story relates how Akbar visited Child Krishna at His home in Gokul, where He had the vision of both Shri Gusainji being rocked in a cradle by Shri Krishna and then Shri Gusainji swaying Child Krishna!

As a young boy, Shri Gusainji used to play the vina to awaken Shri Nathji every morning and again to soothe Him when the Blessed Lord retired for the night. When the tips of his fingers hardened from playing the vina, Shri Gusainji realized that they might cause Shri Nathji discomfort while he adorned Him, and that prompted him to discontinue playing the instrument. His every thought and action was for Shri Krishna's delight. His own devotional practice became the model for all of his followers to emulate.

Shri Gusainji also brought together the eight legendary Ashta Chhap poets and entrusted them with the seva of singing the glories of Shri Krishna's lilas before Shri Nathji and Shri Navanita Priyaji. Four of the poets, Kumbhandas, Surdas, Paramananda Das and Krishnadas were initiated by Shri Vallabhacharya, while Govinda Swami, Chita Swami, Chaturbhujadas and Nandadas were Shri Gusainji's disciples.

Shri Gusainji was fifteen when his father left this world. He married his first wife, Rukminiji, in 1533 CE. She left her body in 1560 after bearing six sons and four daughters. Shri Gusainji's seventh son was born from his second wife, Padmavati, whom he married in 1568. He also adopted an eighth son, Tulsidas, who served as his water carrier.

Shri Gusainji travelled extensively and made many disciples. The bulk of his life story is found in the accounts of his 252 followers. Among his disciples were kings, ministers, the rich and poor. Pandits, people of all castes, Muslims, sadhus and even a robber all became his great devotees. He uplifted his followers by his mere presence. Shri Vitthalnathji's pilgrimages spanned a forty year period and were largely focused in Gujarat. In 1557 CE Shri Gusainji decided to move from his home in Adel by the confluence of the Yamuna and Ganges Rivers to Gokul on the banks of the Yamuna River. In the stories of Shri Gusainji's 252 Vaishnava disciples, the following account is given:

Once, Emperor Akbar asked Birbal, "How can I find God?"

Birbal went to Vrindavan and gathered many answers to the ruler's question from the saints there, but Akbar remained dissatisfied. In search of the perfect answer, Birbal visited many gurus in Vrindavan and relayed to the Emperor what they said, but Akbar was not pleased with anyone's teaching and rebuked him, "You had better find a good answer to my question; otherwise I will loot your house."

That evening when Birbal returned home, full of anxiety, his daughter asked, "What is wrong?"

"I cannot pacify this Emperor."

"Tell me the problem, perhaps I can help."

"The Emperor demands to know how he can meet God. I have conveyed to him the teachings of many Vrindavan pandits and Swamis, but he is not pleased with their teachings. Now he threatens me. I am overwhelmed. What should I do?"

Birbal's daughter calmly replied, "Have you been to see Shri Gusainji?"

"No."

"You will not get the correct answer until you see him. Only God understands Godly things. Now go to Gokul and stop worrying."

Birbal reached Gokul in the early afternoon and waited until Shri Gusainji came out of seva. Birbal bowed before the guru and explained, "Emperor Akbar wants to know how he can meet God."

Shri Gusainji replied, "The answer to that question will be revealed when I meet the Emperor. Only then will his doubts be removed. Tell him I have his answer."

After Birbal told the Emperor what Shri Gusainji had said, Akbar thought, "I will go there alone." He set out for Gokul before sunrise on horseback, disguised so that no one would recognize him. He reached Gokul just as Shri Gusainji was going to the Yamuna River to bathe and perform his midday prayers.

When the Emperor bowed to him, Shri Gusainji recognized him and told everyone else step aside. "What do you wish to know?" Shri Gusainji asked.

"How can I find God?"

"Just as you have found me." Shri Gusainji replied.

In this world, the Emperor is the most important man. If you want to meet him, you must please many people below him. Even then, if it is not the Emperor's wish, he will not meet with you. If you make many plans, the royal meeting may occur, but only after surmounting numerous difficulties. If on the other hand, he wishes to meet with you, then you can be before him in a moment, and he will be eager to see you!

In a similar way, the soul who desires to find the Lord thinks and ponders for a long time about how to find Him, but still He remains illusive. When the blessed Lord resolves, "I want to meet this soul," there is no delay in the reunion.

The Emperor was extremely pleased to hear Shri Gusainji's words and praised him, "People call you Kanhaiya (Krishna), and you truly are. Now please ask something of me. I am very delighted with you."

Shri Gusainji responded, "I do not desire anything."

The Emperor insisted, "Bless me and allow me the opportunity to serve you in some way." Akbar prostrated himself before Shri Vitthalnathji and later presented the bhakti master with a swift Arabian horse. Shri Gusainji rode that horse along the twenty kilometer path from Gokul, where Shri Navanita Priyaji resided, to Shri Nathji's temple and his other home in Jatipura.[27]

Shri Gusainji blessed the poet Chaturbhujadas with the divine vision of Shri Krishna's Lila and brought the Muslim poet Rasakhan before Shri Nathji. He liberated a ghost, turned a snake into a god, and by making Chita Swami's rotten coconut ripe, inspired him toward grace filled devotion. Shri Gusainji's chewed betel nut transformed the mute Gopaldas into an ocean of poetic verse. With his blessing, the songs of the court singer Tansen became devotional. He initiated the Muslims Alikan and his daughter Pirajadi and made their devotion to Shri Krishna so exalted that Pirajadi danced with Krishna while her father played the drum. All that was needed was his blessing. Shri Gusainji knew what each disciple required, and the bhakti master was ever intent on connecting divine souls to their blissful source.

The following account demonstrates Shri Gusainji's love for the bhaktas. One day he joyfully mentioned to his wife, Shri Rukminiji that his bhaktas represented all the various parts of his own body. She questioned, "Which part of your body is your disciple Chachaji?"

Shri Gusainji responded, "Chachaji is the pupil of my eye." Later, when Chachaji stubbed his toe, Shri Gusainji's eyes began to hurt. When Rukminiji asked him why his eyes hurt, he replied, "Chachaji is in pain." Shri Gusainji's eyes recovered once Chachaji's toe was better.

Shri Gusainji was a brilliant devotional teacher whose approach to bhakti was refined and unique. He taught one follower, "If the black bee cannot make it to its beloved water lotus, it remains content. Its love for the lotus enables it to withstand every pleasure and pain. Yet when the black bee that is full of bhava reaches the water lotus, the infinite bliss it receives at that moment is indescribable." Shri Gusainji's followers composed many poems in his honor. Manika Chanda praised,

> In the four eras, You protect the words of the Vedas.
> Whenever dharma weakens,
> > You take on a divine form.
> In the Satya age You were the divine boar
> > who killed the demon Hiranyaksha.
> In the Treta age You appeared as Rama
> > and dispatched Ravana.
> In Dwarpa, You appeared in Vraj as Krishna,
> > and Indra fell at Your feet.
> You killed Kamsa and removed
> > the burden of the world.
> Now You have appeared as Vallabh's son
> > and disproved the Mayavadan philosophy.
> Manika Chanda says, "I gaze upon Krishna,
> > now appearing as Shri Gusainji."

There was no telling where Shri Gusainji's blessings would fall. When Shri Gusainji first came to his disciple Bhaila's house, he initiated everyone in the family. When he was about to give the mute boy Gopaldas mantra, Shri Gusainji asked Bhaila who he was. At that time Gopaldas was nine. Bhaila answered, "He is the husband of my daughter Gomati."

Shri Gusainji laughed and said, "Gomati is a river, and her husband is the ocean. This boy cannot even speak! What type of match is this?"

Bhaila prayed, "Through your grace he will become an ocean."

Shri Gusainji placed Gopaldas on his lap and put some of his chewed betel nut into the boy's mouth. Gopaldas' mind was immediately purified; the young boy bowed to Shri Gusainji and sang:

I bow to Shri Gusainji,
who is beautiful like a fresh rain-filled cloud,
lovely as a Tamal tree.[28]

Shri Gusainji then said, "Gopaldas, sing of Shri Mahaprabhuji." The boy again bowed to Shri Gusainji and began.

By simply remembering
the son of Shri Lakshman,
Shri Mahaprabhu Vallabhacharya,
all bad karmas are erased.[29]

Shri Gusainji said, "Gomati's husband has become an ocean." He blessed him again, and the young boy composed the famous set of nine poems called the *Vallabhakhyan*.

Shri Gusainji also had great love for satsang – sacred discourse with his followers. Late one night when Shri Gusainji came out into his courtyard, his disciple Chachaji happened to be standing there, and they began to discuss some secret devotional matter. They both became so absorbed in Krishna bhava that they were unaware of their physical existence. Shri Gusainji forgot about the heavy pitcher of water he was holding, while Chachaji was unaware that he should have taken the pitcher from his guru's hand. The next day Shri Gusainji remained completely immersed in the bhava of their satsang, while Chachaji did not return his bodily senses for three days!

Shri Gusainji brought souls to the Path and granted them divine experiences. Often, all that was required was the sight of the bhakti master. When Muraridas saw Shri Gusainji taking his bath at Mani Kiran ghat, he was so enchanted that he stood perfectly still for twenty minutes just gazing at him. Shri Gusainji knew him to be a divine soul and accepted him as a disciple. When his disciples realized Shri Gusainji's true divinity, his Lila form, their devotion flourished.

Most of all, Shri Gusainji loved the bhaktas who had pure devotion. It was more important than practice or even purity. Even the simple-minded found the exalted position. In the accounts of his 252 followers we find this interesting account about the younger Patel brother.

The younger Patel brother was so simple-minded that he did not even know Shri Gusainji's name. One day he thought, "I will sit next to my guru, but I do not even know his name. I wonder if I should bow to him?"

At that moment, Shri Gusainji's third son, Shri Bal Krishnaji came before his father and respectfully requested, "Uncle, come for your meals."

Hearing Bal Krishna's words, the younger brother bowed before Shri Gusainji and said, "Today I have learned your name. Your name is 'Uncle.'"

Shri Gusainji was pleased and only saw his straightforward and pure bhava. Everyone was amused with Patel. Shri Gusainji mentioned to his bhaktas, "I have a new nephew, and he has come here to call me Uncle."

Whenever the younger brother came to Shri Gusainji he called out to him, "Uncle!" before bowing. When Shri Gusainji saw him, he would say, "He is coming here just to call me 'Uncle.'"

One day another bhakta told Patel, "The man you call 'Uncle' is Shri Vitthalnathji Gusainji. Use his proper name."

Patel replied, "I don't believe you. What you have just told me will upset my uncle."

On the following day, when Patel came to see Shri Gusainji, he bowed to him and called out, "Uncle, this bhakta told me not to call you Uncle. I can't remember the name he told me; it was so long my tongue could not say it, so I will just call you 'Uncle.'"

Shri Gusainji replied, "Patel, call me the name you can pronounce."[30]

One day Shri Gusainji decided to take sanyasa and become a renunciate. His child Krishna, Shri Navanita Priyaji, knowing of Shri Gusainji's intentions, informed him that He was also taking sanyasa and dyed all of His own clothes saffron, the color of a renunciate. At that moment, Shri Gusainji renounced the idea of taking sanyasa. In the Path of Grace, renunciation is developed by loving Krishna and by always remaining before Him.

Shri Vitthalnathji remained a devotionally inspired Vedic householder and made arrangements for a smooth succession, distributing his wealth amongst his seven sons. He arranged for the daily seva of the Krishna svarupas that had been worshipped since Shri Vallabhacharya's time. All of his sons received the rights to worship Shri Nathji, and the other seven svarupas were distributed among his seven sons, who went on to carry forth his teachings into the world.

In 1586 CE Shri Vitthalnathji walked into a cave on the Govardhan Hill with his disciple Govinda Swami, after giving his shawl with which to perform his last rites to his eldest son, Shri Girdharji. He then entered into Shri Krishna's eternal Lila with his body. Shri Vitthalnathji's descendants maintain the spiritual glory and dignity of the Path of Grace to this day.

5.
THE VALLABHACHARYA LINEAGE

Shri Gusainji writes in *Sarvottama Stotra*, 108 names in praise of his father, Shri Vallabhacharya, "He created His own family lineage to promote devotion in the world. He is a father and has established his unlimited greatness in His own lineage."

There are two types of guru-disciple lineages: *bindu* and *nada*. In nada lineages, the guru chooses one of his disciples to take over his position after his death. In the bindu lineage, succession is hereditary, from father to son. The Path of Grace is a bindu lineage. All past and present day lineage holders in the Path of Grace are direct descendants of Shri Gusainji and his seven sons, Shri Girdharji, Shri Govindaji, Shri Bal Krishnaji, Shri Gokulnathji, Shri Raghunathji, Shri Yadunathji and Shri Ghanshyamji.

Shri Vitthalnathji's first wife, Shri Rukminiji, gave birth to six sons. Her eldest son, Shri Girdharji was born in 1540 CE in Adel. Shri Girdharji married Bhaminiji and had three sons. He was known in Akbar's court as 'Jati.' The town of Jatipura in Vraj, where Shri Nathji's temple was originally located, is named after him. He loved solitude and often spent his time in a cave in Kamar, in a remote part of Vraj. He was a great scholar and worshipped Shri Krishna in his forms of Shri Nathji, Shri Navanita Priyaji as well as Shri Mathureshji. He left this world by entering into mouth of his Krishna svarupa, Shri Mathureshji, when the blessed Lord yawned.

Shri Vitthalnathji's second son, Shri Govindaji, was born in 1542 CE. He married Shri Rani and had four sons. He worshipped Shri Krishna in the form of Shri Vitthalnathji. Shri Govindaji was so attached to Shri Krishna's blessed worship that his marriage ceremony had to be interrupted so he could finish Shri Vitthalnathji's evening worship, as he felt such intense separation from his Lord.

Shri Bal Krishnaji, Shri Vitthalnathji's third son, was born in 1549 CE. He was robust, swarthy and had large lotus-like eyes, such that at home he was called "Lotus-Eyed one." After his studies, he married Shri Kamalavati, who bore him six sons and one daughter. He worshipped Shri Krishna in his form as Shri Dwarkadheesh and spent many years of his life in Gokul. One night he had the darshan of Shri Yamunaji and vowed he would not drink water until he found a Radha svarupa for his Shri Dwarkadheesh. Knowing of his vow, Shri Vitthalnathji gave his son a pair of golden bangles and told him, "These golden bangles will perfectly fit the Radha deity you are so eagerly looking for."

Shri Bal Krishnaji then wandered around Braja until he found his Radha deity and established Her in Shri Dwarkadheesh's seva. Whenever he worshipped Shri Dwarkadheesh, he remained in a divine state of bhava. Once, while he was worshipping Child Krishna in a cradle, Shri Bal Krishnaji became so full of devotion that Child Krishna actually came and sat in his lap. He was a great scholar and wrote many works in Sanskrit.

Shri Vitthalnathji's fourth son was the well-known Shri Gokulnathji. He was born in 1551 CE and married Shri Parvatiji. They had three sons and one daughter. Shri Gokulnathji worshipped Shri Krishna in His form of Shri Gokulnathji, a four-armed golden Krishna. Shri Gokulnathji was very famous and composed wonderful literature in Vrajbhasha and Sanskrit. The stories of Shri Mahaprabhuji

Vallabhacharya's 84 and Shri Gusainji's 252 Vaishnava Disciples, two essential devotional texts in the Pushti Marg, were authored by Shri Gokulnathji. Still today, there are millions of people who revere Shri Gokulnathji and are followers of his house in particular. Many books full of his stories and teachings have been recorded by his followers.

Shri Gokulnathji had great respect for his other brothers. Once when someone stole his youngest brother's Krishna svarupa, Shri Madan Mohanji, Shri Gokulnathji vowed, "The family line of whoever has stolen my brother's Krishna svarupa will not continue."

Someone cautiously mentioned, "Maharaj, what if it was your own son?"

Shri Gokulnathji exclaimed, "Then my own lineage will not continue."

Indeed, it was Shri Gokulnathji's own son who had done the deed. Due to Shri Gokulnathji's curse, for many generations there were no sons born into his line, so that Acharyas had to be adopted from other houses into the fourth seat.

In another well-recorded incident, a sanyasi by the name of Chidrupa convinced Emperor Jahangir to stop all bhaktas from wearing tulasi necklaces and tilaks. Shri Gokulnathji took great efforts to rectify this situation. He himself went to the Emperor's summer palace in Kashmir and eventually convinced the ruler to remove the edict.

Shri Vitthalnathji's fifth son, Shri Raghunathji, was born in 1554 CE in Adel. Once when Shri Raghunathji was just five years old, while Shri Gusainji was absorbed in Shri Nathji's seva, he asked his young son in Sanskrit for the jewelry box. Raghunathji could not understand his father's words. With the grace of Shri Krishna and Shri Mahaprabhuji, he finally understood what his father wanted and brought him the jewelry box, but after this incident, Shri Vitthalnathji decided that in seva, they would speak the local language (Shri Krishna's own language) of Vrajbhasha instead of Sanskrit.

Shri Raghunathji married Shri Janaki in Gokul when he was fifteen and had five sons and one daughter. He was given Shri Gokul Chandramaji for his personal worship. In the morning, Raghunathji would only open his eyes when he could see his father's face. While walking into his father's room one morning with his eyes closed, he bumped into something and hurt himself. Shri Gusainji then painted a self-portrait for him so that he could easily see his father's face after waking every morning.

Shri Yadunathji, Shri Vitthalnathji's sixth son, was born in 1558 CE. He was an expert in Ayurveda, the ancient Indian system of medicine. He married Shri Maharaniji in Gokul when he was about fifteen years old and had five sons and one daughter. His father presented him with a small Child Krishna for his personal worship. Shri Yadunathji brought his Child Krishna to reside with his older brother's Shri Dwarkadheesh, and they all made seva together.

Shri Ghanashyamji, the seventh and youngest son of Shri Vitthalnathji, was born in 1571 by the Acharya's second wife, Shri Padmavatiji. His mother died young, so Shri Ghanashyamji was raised by Shri Girdharji's wife, Shri Bhaminiji. Shri Gusainji was greatly pleased and blessed Bhaminiji that her lineage would always continue. To this day, the family lines of Shri Bhaminiji and Shri Yadunathji are the two that have continued without interruption. The lineages of Shri Gusainji's other sons all had to adopt Acharyas into their house at some point. Shri Ghanashyamji worshipped Shri Madan Mohanji and married Krishnavati. They had two sons and a daughter. Shri Ghanashyamji composed literature in Vrajbhasha and Sanskrit.

Shri Harirayaji, the grandson of Shri Gusainji's second son, Shri Govindaji, was a prolific writer and a important teacher in the Path of Grace. He was born in Gokul in 1591 CE to Shri Kalyanrayaji. Shri Gusainji's blessings over Shri Kalyanrayaji manifested in his son, Shri Harirayaji, who became the only other Acharya in the lineage after Mahaprabhu Shri Vallabhacharya to be honored with the title 'Mahaprabhu.' Shri Mahaprabhu Harirayaji took initiation from Shri Gokulnathji when he was eight years old and learned the seva and teachings of the lineage from him. When there was disturbance from local Muslim rule, Shri Harirayaji moved to Kimnor in Rajasthan, just outside of the current town of Nathdvara. Shri Harirayaji was a very humble Acharya who had many direct experiences of Shri Nathji. It is recorded that if there were ever any mistakes in Shri Nathji's seva, Shri Nathji would appear to Shri Harirayaji. Then Shri Harirayaji would travel to Shri Nathji's temple and correct whatever mistake was made in the blessed worship. Shri Harirayaji was father to four sons.

Bhaktas came from distant parts of India to hear Shri Harirayaji's teachings. They would often become so inspired by hearing his words that they would start to sing and dance. Shri Harirayaji lived for about 125 years and composed an amazing ocean of devotional literature which has enriched the devotional forms of the Path of Grace. His famous teaching, *Shiksha Patra*, contains forty-one letters of grace filled instructions which he wrote to his younger brother, Shri Gopeshwarji. These letters contain the essence of the Path. The forty-one letters as well as Shri Gopeshwarji's commentaries on them are reviewed daily in the gatherings of bhaktas. Shri Harirayaji's own commentary on the 252 and 84 Vaishnava stories reveal foundational teachings of the lineage and illuminate the deeper devotional meanings of the bhaktas' life stories.

Shri Harirayaji's extensive literature covers every topic of the Path of Grace. He wrote in Vrajbhasha, Panjabi,

Gujarati and Marvadi as well as Sanskrit. He also composed many poems under the name "Rasika Pritama." He gave importance to experiencing bhava for the Blessed Lord. His wife, Sundarvanta also composed literature in Vrajbhasha and Gujarati. Shri Harirayaji embodies the spirit of the lineage; without examining his writings, one cannot truly understand the Path of Grace.

Another amazing personality in the Path of Grace was Shri Goswami Purushottamji Maharaja, who was born in 1724 CE. At the age of six, after reciting the 108 names of Shri Vallabhacharya, Shri Mahaprabhu Vallabhacharya appeared before Shri Purushottamji and gave him the gift of wisdom. Shri Purushottamji is believed to have written approximately 900,000 works! He was a master of all scriptures and lineages and wandered around India with bullock carts stacked full of books. He discussed scriptures with pundits wherever he went and could never be defeated. Later in his life, he moved to Surat, where he worshipped Bal Krishnaji, but he left his body in his birthplace, Gokul.

Shri Vallabhacharya's direct lineage is considered to be divine. In his teaching, *The Paths of Grace, Mundane Flow and Lawful Limitations*, Shri Vallabhacharya writes,

> *The creation of grace filled souls is strictly for the loving service of the blessed, blissful Lord. There is no remarkable difference between the Lord's form, His incarnation, the markings on His body, His virtues, and the bhaktas' souls, bodies and actions.*

This teaching applies to his lineage as well as to his followers. The Vallabhacharya lineage has been full of incarnated, enlightened beings. Their contributions to the bhakti teachings, music and grace filled lifestyle have been enormous. In accordance with Shri Vallabhacharya's pure non-dualist system, which views the world as full of Krishna, the Vallabh lineage clearly contains the Krishna essence. We find many stories about Vaishnavas and others who have beheld the various forms of Shri Krishna within Shri Vallabhacharya and his descendants.

The lineage holders give initiation to their disciples in the Path of Grace and establish Krishna's seva in their disciples' homes. They also transmit the sacred teachings of the lineage. To this day the lineage holders are poets, pundits, musicians, Sanskritists, as well as experts in Vedant. Their greatest virtue is their attachment to Shri Krishna's seva. They follow in the footsteps of Shri Vallabhacharya, who referred to himself as *Krishna Das* – a devout follower of Shri Krishna.

To understand the pulse of the lineage, I feel that it is necessary to have contact and teachings directly from the lineage holders. They hold in their blood and hearts the necessary empowerments for understanding the nature of grace and grace filled Shri Krishna. There is also great diversity among the lineage holders, which has created innovations in worship and outlook, as well as from time to time, difference in opinions. Shri Vallabhacharya's family contributions to the devotional dharma truly have no equal. They have maintained the bhakti spirit of Shri Vallabhacharya and have passed it on to other bhaktas, creating divine awareness for over twenty generations.

The homes of lineage holders are abodes of Krishna worship. The lineage holders are affectionately called *Balaks* – or children, reflecting their pure and innocent natures. On a personal note, my entrance and education in the Path of Grace was due to the graceful kindness of His Holiness Goswami Shri Prathameshji Maharaj. He was the head of the first seat and embodied the lineage within his being. His forefathers were all steeped in the modes of seva and teachings. To find a guru with such spiritual expertise was for me a rare gift. It was my good fortune that I came into contact with His Holiness. My debt remains to the entire Vallabhacharya lineage as well as to their followers.

6.
THE ASHTA CHHAP KRISHNA POETS

The eight devotionally inspired bhakta poets known as the Ashta Chhap reside permanently in the heart of the Path of Grace. Four of them – Surdas, Paramananda Das, Kumbhandas and Krishnadas – were Shri Vallabhacharya's disciples, while Chaturbhujadas, Nandadas, Chita Swami and Govinda Swami were initiated by Shri Gusainji. Their songs are sung daily in every Pushti home of worship. Their divine lives continue to inspire us all towards the Blessed Path, which they each experienced in direct, intimate and unique ways. These abbreviated accounts of the eight great poets' lives are drawn from two texts, the *84-* and *252-Vaishnava Stories*, as recounted by Shri Gokulnathji.

SURDAS

Surdas was born in 1479 CE to a Sarasvat Brahmin and lived near Delhi, in a town called Sinhim. He was blind from birth. His father was greatly pained over the situation and thought to himself, "First the Creator made me poor, and now He has given me a blind child! Who will look after him? A person born with no eyes is called blind, not 'Sura – the sun!'" No one in Surdas' home loved him – not his mother, father, nor his siblings. They thought, 'What kind of a son has no eyes?' and so they didn't even talk to him.

One day a wealthy man from the village gave Surdas' father a gift of two gold coins. That night the coins disappeared, to the utter grief of Surdas' mother and father. Surdas saw the futility of their grief and told them, "Why are you agonizing and suffering over this worldly problem? You should serve and remember the Lord – then everything will be just fine."

Hearing this unwelcome advice, his parents reacted sharply, "Since the very moment you were born, Sur, we have spent our lives in suffering. We have not known a single happy moment since then. Yesterday, the Lord gave us two gold coins, and now they too have disappeared!"

Surdas replied, "If you promise not to keep me here, I will tell you where your coins are. But do not follow me after I leave, and don't ever ask me to live in your house again."

When they found the coins exactly where Surdas had indicated, his family realized that Surdas had developed great powers and tried to convince him to stay home. The blind boy refused and left his home. He became a renunciate and began to live by a nearby lake. Surdas gathered a large following and impressed people with his ability to tell the future and see distant events.

One day Surdas awoke to the truth that he had truly attained nothing spiritual and left his ashram and most of his followers, making his way towards Vrindavan. Along the way, he stopped at Go Ghat by the Yamuna River, where he met his guru, Shri Vallabhacharya. The guru opened Surdas' eyes and heart to Shri Krishna's Lila. After his initiation, Surdas immediately sang,

> *Now I have no taste for petty emotions;*
> *my longings lie in the reservoir*
> *of the Lord's lotus feet.*

Shri Vallabhacharya appointed Surdas as one of Shri Nathji's temple singers. Surdas sang of Shri Krishna's childhood and amorous lilas. His writings covered all spiritual topics and Surdas became an ocean of devotional poetry. He left everything mundane. Reflecting on his past life, he sang, *"I've danced enough, Gopal! I've worn a shirt of lust and fury – around my neck, a necklace of worldliness!"*

When Emperor Akbar heard one of Surdas' poems he went to Mathura to find the poet. When he asked the blind poet to sing his glories, Surdas told him,

> *There's not a vacant place in my mind and heart.*
> *How could another enter my heart*
>   *in the place of Nanda's Son?*

The Emperor was impressed with Surdas and offered him several villages and a great deal of wealth, but Surdas didn't accept any of it. Akbar told Surdas to ask for whatever he wanted, to which the poet responded, "From today onward, don't ever call on me again, and don't try to meet me."

Later Akbar tried to collect some of Surdas' poems. One poet produced a poem claiming it to be Surdasji's, but Akbar suspected it was a forgery. The Emperor placed it in some water along with a real poem by Surdas. The fake poem sank, while Surdas' poem floated on the water. Surdas was a true saint.

One day, Shri Gusainji's sons tested the blind poet by adorning Child Krishna, Shri Navanita Priyaji with only two strings of pearls around His head, pearl arm bands, a pearl belt, anklets and necklaces made of pearls, earrings, a tilak, nose ring, but no clothes! Then they brought Surdas into the temple then asked him, "Surdasji! Behold the Lord and sing a kirtan." Surdas immediately sang,

Just look!
Hari is totally nude!
He is adorned with pearls and no clothes.
The beauty of His form creates waves.

Another story found in Surdas' life story relates how one day his assistant, Gopal got distracted and forgot to bring a glass of water to Surdas along with his meal. While eating, Surdas suddenly began to choke. With food stuck in his throat and unable to call out for help, Surdas panicked. Knowing of his plight, Shri Nathji left His temple and brought Surdas some water from His own golden water pitcher. Surdas drank from the pitcher. When his assistant returned, Surdas reprimanded him, "How can you call yourself Gopal? Only Shri Nathji is the true Gopal. He protected me today. You have done a terrible thing to cause Shri Nathji such hardship. For my sake, Shri Nathji had to come with His pitcher of water."

Later Shri Gusainji mentioned to Surdas, "Today Shri Nathji has truly blessed you."

Surdas replied, "It all happened through your grace. Otherwise, how would the Lord have taken note of a fallen soul like myself? Shri Nathji accepts us through the graceful intercession of Shri Mahaprabhu Vallabhacharya."

Shri Gusainji praised Surdas, "You are really a great devotee. Only pure-hearted souls can possess such humility."

Another account in Surdas' life story tells of a grocer who was very greedy and attached to his household life. The grocer's shop was just at the foot of the Govardhan Hill, but he never went to have Shri Nathji's darshan and had not taken initiation from Shri Gusainji. Every morning the grocer would ask the first Vaishnava who came down from the temple what Shri Nathji was wearing that day. When other bhaktas came to his shop, the grocer would exclaim, "What amazing ornamentation Shri Nathji wore today! What a divine darshan!"

Just to impress the Vaishnavas and increase business, the grocer wore the Vaishnava *tilak* mark on his forehead and the sacred tulsi necklace. In front of the Vaishnavas, he would tell stories of Krishna's divine love. Everyone was pleased with this and, thinking him to be a real devotee, purchased goods from him.

One day Surdas confronted him on his untruths and eventually brought the misguided grocer before Shri Nathji. Surdas gave him teachings in verse:

Today work, tomorrow work,
*   and the day after, you'll work again.*
The first day you worked so much,
*   you lost interest in the Lord's feet.*
While waking you work, and you work in your sleep,
*   and after that you'll die.*
Leave your work and remember Shyam!
*   Sur proclaims, 'This is true shelter.'*

Another time when the poet Paramananda Das and ten other bhaktas came to meet Surdas, the blind poet greeted them with a song,

A moment with Krishna's bhaktas
*   surpasses the pleasures of a million heavens*
*   and liberations by the billions....*
The day saints arrive in your life,
The fruit of a billion sacred baths
*   is achieved by their very sight....*
Says Surdas, "Love those who make you remember the Lord."

After Surdas had sang in Shri Nathji's service for many years, he realized that the Lord wished for him to return to His eternal realm. Surdas considered, "I have vowed to compose 125,000 poems before leaving this world. So far, I have composed 100,000. If it is the Lord's wish, I will compose twenty five thousand more poems. Then I will cast off this physical body."

Just then, Shri Nathji appeared directly before Surdas, saying, "Surdasji, your heart's desire to compose 125,000 poems has already been completed. I have finished the remaining 25,000 poems – look in your book."

Surdas then asked one Vaishnava to look through his poetry book. He found amongst Surdas' poems 25,000 new poems signed 'Sur Shyam.' The Vaishnava told Surdas, "Yesterday there were no poems signed by Sur Shyam, but today, in the middle of your other poems, there are twenty five thousand new poems bearing that name! They encompass all the lilas of the Lord."

Surdas then bowed to Shri Nathji and said, "Through Your grace, the desires of my heart have been fulfilled. Now, I will follow Your commands."

The Lord replied, "Now return to My Lila and experience the nectar of My love."

Surdas then went to Parasoli by the Moon Lake, bowed down towards the flag on top of Shri Nathji's temple and lay down to sleep. Some bhaktas came to greet him, and he sang a now famous poem about his devotion to his guru:

I have firm faith in Shri Vallabh's lotus feet.
Without the moonbeams that shine from His toenails,
*   the entire world falls into darkness.*
In this age of struggle, there is no other practice
*   by which to attain true liberation*
Sings Sur, I may be blind in two ways,
*   but I am His priceless servant.*

In his last moments Surdasji gave a final teaching,

Worship love-filled Krishna
 with the devotional mood of the Gopis.
What is the point of your million practices
 if you do not serve Him with love?

Shri Gusainji then asked him, "Surdasji, where is your mind now?" At that moment, Surdas sang a poem about Shri Radha:

Young Radha,
 I rejoice over You, for You have chosen
  to love Krishna....

Surdasji sang one last song about Radha's "maddened Khanjan-bird eyes, so lovely and unsteady," and then fixed his mind on the forms of the divine Couple, cast off his mortal body, and entered into the Lord's Lila.

Surdas has four names. Shri Mahaprabhuji called him 'Sur,' which means 'warrior.' In battle, a warrior never takes one step back; he moves ahead and faces every foe. In that way, Surdas' devotion continually progressed day by day.

Shri Gusainji called him 'Surdas.' The attitude of loving service, 'Das bhava,' never diminishes. As Surdas' experiences of the Lord's Lila increased, so did his humility; he never developed egotism or pride. Surdas' third name is 'Surajdas.' Surdasji composed seven thousand poems in praise of Shri Swaminiji, which reveal many divine moods. Shri Swaminiji Herself then said of Surdas, 'He is Suraj – the sun!' Just as the sun lights the world, so Surdas illuminated Her divine form. The twenty five thousand poems which Shri Nathji composed for Surdas were all signed with the name, 'Sur Shyam.' In this way, Surdas' four different names can be found in the signature of his poems.

The highest teaching revealed in Surdas' life story is that there is no position equal to humility and no dharma equal to kindness towards others. Surdas undertook such great efforts for the sake of that grocer, arranging for his initiation and upliftment. That is why Shri Mahaprabhu, Shri Gusainji, the Vaishnavas, and everyone else were pleased with Surdas. If anyone came to Surdas with a question, he would lovingly explain the principles of the devotional Path and direct their thoughts toward Krishna. Out of a billion accomplished devotees, it would be difficult to find one equal to Surdas.

PARAMANANDA DAS

Paramananda Das, who was known as 'Paramananda Swami' before his initiation into the Path of Grace, was born into a Brahmin family in Kanoj. After his parents lost all of their wealth, they told him, "Son, we don't have enough money to marry you."

He replied, "I do not wish to marry. What is the use of collecting money? What did you attain with all your wealth, which you have now lost? The reward of wealth is using it to feed the bhaktas and Brahmins." Paramananda Das surrounded himself with kirtan singers and became extremely talented in the art of singing. As his fame spread from town to town, he gathered disciples of his own and became known as Paramananda Swami. Once when he was in Prayag for the Maha Makar bath, someone mentioned his name to Shri Vallabhacharya. The master commented, "Paramananda Das is a divine soul, so it is only natural that he has such talent."

Shri Vallabhacharya had a disciple named Kapur Kshatri who loved music. When Kapur heard about the great singer, he decided to go to Prayag to hear that night's concert.

He listened as Paramananda Swami sang,

O friend, I want to meet Krishna
    the Son of Nanda.
Since I saw His eyes,
    He has stolen my heart away.
I cannot sleep; the length of the night
    is beyond measure.
I anxiously await the coming morn.

Paramananda Swami sang for the entire night. Kapur left early that morning after greeting the poet with, "Jai Shri Krishna." While Paramananda Swami slept, in a dream he saw Kapur at the previous night's performance. Krishna as Shri Navanita Priyaji was sitting in Kapur's lap, listening to the kirtan! Shri Navanita Priyaji laughed and said to Paramananda Swami, "Today, after so many days, I have finally heard your singing. Kapur, Shri Mahaprabhuji's blessed disciple, came to hear you, and I accompanied him."

When Paramananda Swami awoke, the beauty of Shri Navanita Priyaji's form, lovely as a million love gods, shimmered in his eyes. Knowledge filled his heart, and he became anxious to see Lord Krishna again. That morning he took the first boat across to Adel, where he saw Shri Mahaprabhuji performing his morning sandhya prayers. At that moment, the poet had a vision of Shri Mahaprabhuji as the remarkable divine form of Shri Krishna Himself. It was as Shri Gusainji explained in *Vallabhashtak*, that Shri Mahaprabhuji "actually is none other than Shri Krishna." Paramananda Swami was astonished by the vision and became speechless. Just then, Shri Mahaprabhu called out, "Paramananda Das, sing something about Shri Krishna's Lila!"

How long has it been since Gopal left?
He is the wealth of Paramananda Swami's life....
I can't forget those lotus-petal eyes!
Now I shed constant tears.

Paramananda Swami sang such poems of separation, as he had not yet experienced the nectar-mood of union with Shri Krishna. After Shri Vallabhacharya initiated him, any obstructive ignorance within Paramananda Swami was dispelled. When Shri Mahaprabhuji explained to him the tenth canto of the Shrimad Bhagavatam, he gained direct experience of Shri Krishna's form as Shri Navanita Priyaji. All of the lilas described in that sacred text arose clearly in his heart, and he began to sing of Krishna's childhood lilas. Of all Shri Mahaprabhuji's grace filled disciples, only Paramananda Swami and Surdas are called 'oceans.' Their songs, like the oceans, have no limits. One day he sang,

O friend. The beautiful, lotus-eyed Shyam
is rocking in a cradle.
All the Gokul Gopis are singing of His childhood lilas....
His curly locks are like lines of black bees....
Paramananda Swami nourishes
love for young Gopal.

Later Paramananda Swami lived with Shri Mahaprabhuji at his home in Adel, at the confluence of the Ganga and Yamuna Rivers. There, Shri Mahaprabhuji told Paramananda Swami, "Sing poems throughout the day for my Child Krishna, Shri Navanita Priyaji. This will be your seva."

Paramananda Swami wrote new poems daily and sang them to Shri Navanita Priyaji from dawn to dusk. During the times he was not singing in the temple, he would go before Shri Mahaprabhuji and sing about Shri Krishna's Vraj lilas.

Shri Vallabhacharya understood that Paramananda Swami wanted to visit Shri Krishna's land of Vraj and arranged to take him there, along with a few disciples. When they passed through the poet's home town of Kanoj, Paramananda Das requested Shri Mahaprabhuji to visit his home. There he sang a poem which began with the line, "*O Krishna, I remember Your Lila.*"

Upon hearing those words, Shri Vallabhacharya became so engrossed in Krishna's divine pastimes that he fell unconscious. He remained in a devotional trance for three days, completely unaware of the physical world. Shri Mahaprabhu remained unconscious for three days because Shri Krishna's Rasa Lila is performed in three main places: the Govardhan Hill (Shri Giriraj), Shri Vrindavan, and Shri Yamunaji. The first day, Shri Mahaprabhuji experienced Krishna's many loving lilas on the Govardhan Hill, where, as Chaturbhujadas has sung, "Krishna and His consort have spent the night in loving plays in a cave in the Govardhan Hill."

On the second day, Shri Mahaprabhuji experienced the bower lilas of Vrindavan, and on the third day he saw the Lord's water dalliance and other plays by the Yamuna River. On the fourth day he came back to this earth, in order to teach devotion, bring many souls to the shelter of the Lord, and to give them the experience of the nectar of Krishna's lilas. Paramananda Swami was troubled and decided, "I will not sing songs of separation in front of Shri Mahaprabhuji again." He sang,

Friend, I sing of auspicious bliss!
*   Krishna is the wish fulfilling jewel of Gokul.*
Whatever you ask for is received....

My friend, let's go and live
        in Krishna's town of Nandagam.
There we will laugh and play in the cowpen with
                the Moon of Vraj, Shri Krishna....
My eyes are like the fish,
        thirsting every moment for His sight.
Sings Paramananda Das,
        "This is a difficult love."

Paramananda Das requested, "Maharaj! Before, I thought I was a Swami – a spiritual master, and made many followers. Now, I am your *Das* – your servant. I made disciples out of my ignorance. Now accept and liberate them."

When they arrived in Gokul, by the banks of the Yamuna River, Shri Mahaprabhuji taught Paramananda Das his *Yamunashtakam*, a Sanskrit prayer in praise of Shri Yamunaji: "*I joyfully bow to Shri Yamunaji, the Giver of all divine powers....*" After hearing the Yamunashtakam, Shri Yamunaji's divine form enlightened Paramananda Das' heart, and he began to sing her glories:

Shri Yamunaji,
May I receive this grace:
To remain close to You every day,
        singing the glories of Rama and Krishna.

Shri Mahaprabhuji was pleased to hear Paramananda Das' praises of Shri Yamunaji and gave him the direct vision of Shri Krishna's divine childhood lilas in Gokul. He sang of how "the Gopis come to Queen Yashoda's house and gaze upon Shri Krishna's lotus face to dispel the anguish of separation they have felt all day."

The Path of Grace

After having the darshan of Gokul, Paramananda Das became very attached to that town. He later sang to Shri Mahaprabhuji, "Keep me in Gokul, near to your lotus feet, so that I can daily have the sight of Shri Krishna and experience all of His lilas."

Let me live in Vraj
*   and drink Shri Yamunaji's waters.*
To serve Shri Vallabh is my oath.
The Gopis' servant Paramananda Das prays,
"Let me find abundant grace
*   and sing Shri Krishna's glories."*
....This I ask of you Krishna, Balaram's brother:
To have constant love for Your lotus feet
*   and to enjoy the gathering of bhaktas.*

Some time later, Shri Mahaprabhu took Paramananda Das and a group of Vaishnavas from Gokul to the Govardhan Hill. After beholding Shri Nathji, Paramananda Das became very attached to His form. Shri Mahaprabhuji then called to him from inside the temple, "Paramananda Das! Sing something for Shrinathji about the Lila."

Paramananda Das sang,

Mohan the Enchanter has become the son of Nandaraya.
The Supreme Lord, hero of the intimate glade,
*   has incarnated for the benefit of His bhaktas.*
His cheeks are embellished with alligator shaped earrings,
*   His eyes, attractive and wide...*
I have bound my heart to Hari
*   and severed all other ties....*

That night, after drinking milk which had been offered to Shri Nathji, Paramananda Das remained absorbed in the nectar of Krishna's Lila for the entire night, singing:

Upon seeing Shri Radha's full moon face,
an ocean of bliss swells in Krishna's body
and overflows into Vraj and Vrindavan.

His devotional mood continued, as he sang,

What nectar did those Gopis gulp?
Whenever they can get near to Krishna,
they loot both love and passion.
Beholding Krishna's form,
they relinquish all worldly shame.
Sings Paramananda Das,
"The ocean of Vedic restrictions was wiped out!"

Paramananda Das sang many more such poems, and Shri Mahaprabhuji gave him the service of singing poems to Shri Nathji. One day a queen came for Shri Nathji's darshan and insisted upon wearing her veil. She did not heed the advice of her king, who told her, "Krishna is the Lord of Vraj, so women do not veil themselves before Shri Nathji." Shri Mahaprabhuji arranged for the queen to enter the temple first for a private darshan, but Shri Nathji suddenly got down from His throne and opened the temple doors Himself. The crowd awaiting darshan poured in, and in the rush, the queen's clothes were torn from her body. She was greatly embarrassed.

Paramananda Das, who was in the temple singing a poem to Shri Nathji at the time of this incident, sang the following line: "Who plays like that? Madan Gopal doesn't follow anyone's rules."

Shri Mahaprabhuji heard that line and corrected Paramananda Das, "Don't say that. Say it like this: 'How wonderful is His play!'"

One day, Surdas, Kumbhandas, Ramdas and some other bhaktas went together to meet Paramananda Das at his home. When they arrived the poet greeted them:

Come, lovers of Krishna,
adorned with sacred tulsi necklaces
  and enchanting tilak markings.
You all contain the splendor of the three worlds.
What pious deed could I have done
  to allow you to grace my home?
....Hari graces those who have a moment's contact
  with His bhaktas.

Paramananda Das then explained to the bhaktas,

"The Gopis hold the banner of love.
They bring Krishna under the sway of their love....
None can equal the Gopis –
  they offer it all, their minds and bodies, to Hari.
They hold Him in their hearts
  and forever wander with that Enticer.
Shri Krishna meditates upon those Gopis!
He constantly repeats their names
  and forgets everything else.

Paramananda Das was inspired when he heard Shri Gusainji sing of the auspiciousness of Vraj and composed his own poems on that theme:

To utter Krishna's name is auspicious.
  His face is auspicious,

His lotus-like hands are auspicious....
auspicious has become the mind of Paramananda Das.

Once, on the day of Krishna's appearance, *Janmashtami,* Paramananda Das praised the festivities in song:

Today, Krishna is born.
Join in the colorful celebration!
Paramananda Das' Krishna, the Lord of the world,
is now disguised as a cowlad....
Today, Papa Nanda is ecstatic.
The Gopis dance and celebrate boisterously with song....
Supreme Bliss has flooded Gokul
and delights my heart.

Paramananda Das was so transported with bliss that he began to dance and, forgetting the order of the ragas, sang a poem in the midday Saranga raga in the middle of the night! He became so absorbed in love that he fell to the ground unconscious. Shri Gusainji lifted up the poet with his own lotus hands and revived him by reciting a Vedic mantra and sprinkling some water over him. Shri Gusainji commented, "Just as Kumbhandas is perfectly immersed in Krishna's youthful lilas, so Paramananda Das has attained total focus upon Krishna's child lilas."

Paramananda Das then bowed to Shri Gusainji. At the bottom of the Govardhan Hill, he prostrated to Shri Nathji's flag on top of the temple and then proceeded to his hut by the Surabhi Lake. He stopped speaking and became totally absorbed in the nectar of Krishna's appearance festivities. Considering that the time had come to leave his body, he laid down and went to sleep. Shri Gusainji and some bhaktas went to see the poet, who bowed to Shri Gusainji and sang,

Love the Son of Nanda.
In fortune and disaster, He protects.
Through His grace, we live.

While meditating upon the divine Couple, Paramananda Das sang,

The deer-eyed Radha adorns Herself with flowers....
Without Krishna, Her day passes like an eon.
Recollecting Her dalliance with Hari,
love for the dark, lovely Shyam stirs within Her heart.
When the day is over at last and night engulfs the land of Vraj,
She encounters the Mountain Holder, Krishna.
This lovely Vraj maiden is elated
to be with the Master of supreme bliss.

After singing that praise, Paramananda Das left his body and entered into Krishna's eternal Lila. Shri Gusainji then said to all those present, "In the Path of Grace, there are two oceans: one is Surdas, and the other is Paramananda Das. Their hearts are filled with the unfathomable ambrosia of the Lord's Lila and overflow with devotional jewels." Paramananda Das is a vessel of Shri Mahaprabhuji's grace, and Shri Nathji was always pleased with him. His life story can never be fully told. It is beyond words, so what else can be said?

KUMBHANDAS

Kumbhandas lived in Yamunavata but spent a lot of time tending his forefathers' farmlands at Parasoli by the Moon Lake. From childhood, Kumbhandas was unattached to household life. He always spoke the truth, refrained from sin and wrongdoing, and lived the pure and simple life of a

Vrajvasi. When Kumbhandas became a young man, he married a woman from Bahulavan who was ordinary and did not have connection with Shri Krishna's Lila. However, the association of the great devotee Kumbhandas could never be unfruitful and ultimately uplifted her.

When Kumbhandas heard that a great being, Shri Vallabhacharya had arrived in Anyor, he told his wife, "Let's go to Anyor and become Shri Mahaprabhu's followers. With his grace, Shri Krishna will bless us." As Kumbhandas was a divine soul, he became aware of Shri Vallabhacharya's divine form simply by beholding him. Kumbhandas bowed down to the guru and submitted, "I have wandered for so long. Now shower your grace upon me."

Kumbhandas' wife asked, "Maharaj! You are a great soul. Bless me with children."

Shri Mahaprabhuji happily gave his blessing, "Don't worry, you will have seven."

She was very pleased to hear that, but later, Kumbhandas scolded his wife, "Why did you request only that? You would have received the Lord if you had asked for Him."

She bluntly replied, "I requested what I desired. You go ahead and ask for whatever you want." Kumbhandas then remained silent.

Kumbhandas had an exquisite singing voice and sang kirtan beautifully, so Shri Mahaprabhuji told him, "Daily sing kirtans for Shri Nathji, according to the time of day." One morning, Kumbhandas sang,

Krishna!
You promised to visit last night,
> *but You have spent the night somewhere else*
>> *and come here just before sunrise?*
You hastily picked up her blue shawl,
> *leaving Your own yellow garments there.*

Sings Kumbhandas,
"You may be able to hold a mountain,
  but You can't keep a promise!"

Shri Mahaprabhuji commented, "You are very fortunate that from the very start Shri Krishna has blessed you, by the power of His grace, with intimate knowledge of His Lila. You will always remain immersed in that bliss."

Kumbhandas replied, "Maharaj, shower your grace and bless me with the experience of this best of all nectars." Kumbhandas was so enamored by Shri Radha and Krishna's intimate play that he never praised anything beside the union lilas of the divine Couple; he did not sing about Shri Krishna's appearance day, cradle songs or other childhood lilas. He never left the Govardhan Hill, the area of Shri Krishna's intimate play, not even to venture to Gokul, the sacred site of Krishna's infant lilas only twenty kilometers away.

Once when Muslim invaders attacked the area, Shri Nathji told Kumbhandas, "I want to go to the nearby berry thicket at Tond Ghana. Sadu Pande has a buffalo. Bring it here, and I'll climb up onto its back and ride it." As they proceeded to Tond Ghana, Ramdas and Sadu Pande each held onto Shri Nathji on the buffalo while Kumbhandas and Manika Chanda cleared the path ahead. There were a lot of thorns, so they had a very difficult time, and their clothes were all torn. In the middle of the Tond Ghana berry thicket, they came upon a Nikunja bower and a river. Kumbhandas thought, "Shri Nathji wants to hear something amusing," and so he sang,

You really like this berry thicket?
We are stuck with thorns and burrs,
  and our clothes are torn.

Kumbhandas was an intimate bhakta of Shri Nathji and realized that the real reason Shri Nathji wanted to go there was to meet His Beloved Shri Swaminiji. Seeing the intimate lila behind this course of events, he sang,

'Go and speak to the captivating Shyam.
He is sitting amongst a cluster of lotuses
in the shade of a Kadam tree.'
....Hearing the messenger's sweet words,
Radha's heart and body were exhilarated.
Sings Kumbhandas,
"That young lady of Vraj then went to meet
Krishna, the Mountain Holder,
Connoisseur of all nectars."[1]

His poem delighted Shri Nathji. When the Muslim invaders retreated, Shri Nathji rode the buffalo back to the temple, where Kumbhandas again broke into verse,

Glories to You, Krishna,
Who removed the anguish of the residents of Vraj.
Glories to You, Krishna,
adorned with golden garments bright as lightning....
The entire world reveres Your lotus feet.
By the banks of the Yamuna River,
Krishna plays and Kumbhandas prays,
"I bow and take Your shelter."

Once Emperor Akbar sent some men to summon Kumbhandas to his court. Kumbhandas told them, "I am a poor resident of Vraj, but I am no one's servant except Shri

---

[1] This type of poem is called *maan*. In these poems, Krishna's lover becomes annoyed with Krishna and refuses to meet Him. Krishna then sends a Gopi messenger to plead His case.

Krishna's. What work could I possibly have with your Emperor that requires me to go there?"

The guards explained, "If you don't accompany us, the Emperor will have us killed, so please come."

Kumbhandas considered, "Then I must go for their sake." He entered the palace and stood before the Emperor, wearing a ripped shirt, soiled clothes and turban and worn-out shoes. The palace was sweetly scented, inlaid with pearls and jewels, but Kumbhandas' heart was pained. He thought, "It is as if I have arrived in hell, although I am still alive. My place in Vraj is better than this. In Vraj, Krishna Himself plays Lila."

The Emperor spoke, "Baba, you have written many poems about the Lord. Now I would like to hear some. Please sing such a poem for me."

Kumbhandas thought to himself, "This man has forced me here, separating me from my Beloved Lord. It would be good to sing something insulting to him. What can he do to me?" Then Kumbhandas remembered the saying, 'Even if the whole world is his enemy, not a hair can fall from the head of one whom Krishna has accepted.' He then composed a poem and sang it for Akbar.

What can a bhakta possibly gain
    by coming to your palace here in Sikri?
While walking here, my shoes became worn
    and I forgot Hari's name.
Now I am forced to pay homage to a face
    whose mere sight troubles me.
Says Kumbhandas, "Without Lala Giridhar (Shri Nathji)
    this palace is just an abode of lies."

Hearing Kumbhandas' song, Akbar was at first enraged but then reflected, "If Kumbhandas were greedy, he would have praised me. He is clearly only interested in his Lord." He then offered, "Kumbhandas, ask of me whatever you want, and I will do as you say."

Kumbhandas immediately replied, "Never call on me again."

As Kumbhandas walked back to his village, he was overwhelmed with the mood of Shri Krishna's separation and softly sang,

When will these eyes behold Him?
Every charming limb of my superb Shyam
    bestows delight....
Since the day I beheld Him, I've forgotten everything
    and have left my husband and family.
Now, without His sight, I am lost.
    My every limb reels with emptiness....
This infatuation with Krishna is tough on my heart....
Sings Kumbhandas,
    "Krishna knows the core of my love."

Shri Nathji enjoyed Kumbhandas' poetry and praised him, "Kumbhandas, you are a blessed one. Just as you cannot live a moment without Me, so without you, everything seems bland." Their love was truly mutual.

Once during the hot season Raja Mansingh came to Shri Nathji's temple. Rose water was splashed all around the temple. Shri Nathji's body was anointed with sandalwood paste. The air was scented with flower oils and circulated by fans. Seeing Shri Nathji adorned with a light white cotton cloth, a few pearl necklaces and other delicate pearl jewelry, Raja Mansingh was cooled to the core of his being and remarked, "This is the true way to serve the Lord. Here, the Krishna who is spoken about in the Shrimad Bhagavatam has personally appeared as Shri Govardhan Nathji and is happily residing in this temple. It is my great fortune to have this vision." Meanwhile, Kumbhandas was singing:

When I behold Him,
my eyelids don't even blink.
My eyes stick to His every portion.
My heart is swept away.
How to describe what I see?
I cannot utter a single word!
Krishna, the One who begs for curds,
has taken off with my mind.
Kumbhandas knows
"What delightful things Krishna tells the Gopis
when they meet!"

Raja Mansingh later asked, "Who was that singing before Shri Nathji? His singing really got to me; I have never heard anything like it." The next day he went to visit Kumbhandas. Meanwhile, Shri Nathji had appeared in Kumbhandas' fields, and the poet called out to Him, "Baba! Come closer!"

Shri Nathji came and sat in Kumbhandas' lap and affectionately said, "I have come here to tell you something special." At that moment, Raja Mansingh arrived. Shri Nathji quickly got up and ran off to hide behind some nearby trees. Kumbhandas' gaze remained fixed on the spot where Shri Nathji was hiding; he did not even glance at Raja Mansingh. The king watched as Kumbhandas sat on a bundle of grass and applied a tilak to his forehead by looking at his reflection in a bowl of water. He thought to himself, "Kumbhandas is indeed impoverished. He doesn't even have a proper seat or a mirror."

Raja Mansingh then called for a gold mirror studded with costly jewels and presented it to Kumbhandas, "Use this mirror to make your tilak."

Kumbhandas refused, "Where will I keep such a costly mirror? Ours is a thatched roof house made of mud. Someone trying to steal this costly ornament might kill us. I don't want such a thing." The king then offered Kumbhandas gold and even the town of Yamunavata itself, but Kumbhandas refused. The king finally offered to provide lifetime unlimited credit for Kumbhandas at his grocers. "My grocer and I have the same disposition," Kumbhandas replied.

"Tell me where he lives so I can pay him," the king implored.

Kumbhandas motioned toward two distant trees and explained, "Those are my grocers. In the hot season the Karila tree gives me flowers and *tanti* berries, and during winter that Bera tree supplies me with unlimited berries."

Raja Mansingh lauded the poet. "You are blessed. The trees are your grocers! I have seen great renunciates before, but never a renounced householder. There is none equal to you upon the face of the earth." Bowing to Kumbhandas, the king then pleaded, "Please give me some command. I will consider it my great fortune to follow whatever you say."

Kumbhandas then asked, "Will you really do what I say?" When the king promised, Kumbhandas rebuffed him, "Never come to me again, and never talk to me."

After Raja Mansingh left, Kumbhandas' niece complained, "We don't have a single possession. Why didn't you accept anything the king offered?"

"Sit down, you foolish girl!" Kumbhandas reprimanded. "If Shri Nathji hears you, He will be enraged and consider that 'Kumbhandas' niece is a very greedy girl!'"

When Shri Nathji returned to the poet, Kumbhandas overflowed with devotion and sang,

O Krishna! You are the great love of my life.
Never stray from these eyes!
"You are the Holder of the Mountain.
Why were You afraid of that man?"

Shri Nathji then began to explain, "Kumbhandas! Today there is a contest among all of My friends to see who can cook the most delicious meal for Me. Will you also participate?"

Kumbhandas asked, "Is there anything in particular You would like?"

Shri Nathji replied, "Barley porridge, milk, yoghurt, and millet roti breads with pickled tanti berries."

Kumbhandas happily replied, "We have all of those items at home!" As Shri Nathji's other friends arrived with their picnic lunches, Kumbhandas placed all of his offerings close to Shri Nathji. The blessed Lord then tasted all of their treats. Shri Nathji found Kumbhandas' offerings very tasty. As He was enjoying the offerings, Kumbhandas sang,

These tanti berries are the supreme fruit of Vraj.
They can be prepared as a vegetable or pickled
and eaten with millet roti breads.

He reflected, "How fortunate that Shri Nathji told me about the food contest and then gave me the experience of that lila." Shri Nathji truly blessed Kumbhandas. For the rest of the day, Kumbhandas remained absorbed in the supreme joy of that lila, unaware of anything else. When he regained outer awareness later that afternoon, Kumbhandas remembered that he had not yet had Shri Nathji's darshan in the temple. He immediately ran from Parasoli to the Govardhan Hill, his heart filled with divine longing. That evening he sang,

Our eyes met and became four.
Ravaged, I just stood there,
forgetting the shawl covering my breasts....
Love for that Charmer of even the love god
*   surged within me;*
I forgot about my household duties.
Now I am greedy for Krishna's nectar,
*   even if it means transgressing the righteous path....*
Kumbhandas offers his body, mind
*   and absolutely everything else*
*   to the Mountain Holder.*

Once, Shri Hita Harivamsh, Shri Haridas and some other Vaishnava saints from Vrindavan came to meet Kumbhandas, for they had heard that Shri Krishna spoke directly with him. When they asked him to sing something about Shri Radha, he sang,

Young Radha, you embody ultimate fortune.
*   A billion moons could never compare to Your face....*
Radha, You are amazing from head to toe.
*   How long can I keep comparing?*
Even Krishna, the Mountain Holder, declares,
*   'My pleasure lies in beholding Her every second.'*

Hearing Kumbhandas' song, the Vrindavan saints exclaimed, "We have composed many poems about Shri Swaminiji, in which Her beauty had been likened to the moon and other things, but you have compared her face to a billion moons! You saw nothing in this world that could adequately compare to Shri Swaminiji's beauty, and therefore you described Her in this most amazing way."

Once, Shri Gusainji decided to travel to Dwarka with the intention of uplifting the divine souls living in those far away lands, and he asked Kumbhandas to come along. They set out the next day for Gujarat and set up camp for the night just a few kilometers away, at the far end of the Govardhan Hill by Apsara Lake. That afternoon, when Kumbhandas remembered that it was time for Shrinathji's afternoon darshan, his eyes filled with tears, and every hair on his body stood on end in ecstatic bliss. Leaning against a tree just outside of Shri Gusainji's tent, Kumbhandas began to sing softly of his anguish:

How many days have passed
     since I last beheld Him?
....His glance and enchanting smile –
     His elegant dancer's garb!
....Kumbhandas laments,
     "Without Shri Nathji,
          my life is worthless."

     Shri Gusainji overheard Kumbhandas' song of separation. Unable to bear the poet's distress, Shri Gusainji emerged from his tent and saw Kumbhandas' eyes streaming with tears. He declared, "Kumbhandas! Your far-away journey has been completed. Now go back to the temple and see Shri Nathji."

     Once, when Kumbhandas and some other Vaishnavas were sitting with Shri Gusainji, the guru said in a joking mood, "Kumbhandas, how many sons do you have?"

     Kumbhandas replied, "One and a half."

     "I thought you had seven sons!" Shri Gusainji questioned.

     "Maharaj," Kumbhandas explained, "of my seven sons, five are attached to the ways of the world, so I don't count them. I have only one full son, and that is

Chaturbhujadas. Then there is Krishnadas, whom I count as half a son, as he does the seva of tending Shri Nathji's cows."

Krishnadas tended Shri Nathji's cows and did indeed have the darshan of Shri Krishna, but he did not know the secret lilas which the Gopis experience in the state of separation. Therefore, Krishnadas' father considered him to be a half son. Only Chaturbhujadas had experienced the nectars of Shri Krishna's union and separation and was able to use that personal experience in the seva by singing kirtans about Krishna's Lila. That is why Kumbhandas considered him a full-fledged son.

Kumbhandas' son Krishnadas was tending Shri Nathji's cows one day when a tiger attacked one of the cows, and Krishnadas gave up his own life to save the cow. When Kumbhandas heard about his son's death he fell to the ground unconscious. Everyone thought, "He is grieving his son's death."

Shri Gusainji then came and explained, "It is not his son's death that pains Kumbhandas so greatly. He is upset because he will not be able to have Shri Nathji's darshan during *sutak*, the period of observance after the death of a relative."

Shri Gusainji then called out to him, "Kumbhandas! Come tomorrow morning, and I will arrange for you to have Shri Nathji's darshan."

Hearing Shri Gusainji's words, Kumbhandas arose, bowed, and said, Other than you, who could know my heart so well!"

Shri Gusainji assured him, "I know that nothing worldly can affect you."

On one occasion, Shri Gusainji's sons Shri Gokulnathji and Shri Balkrishnaji approached their father and said, "Kumbhandas has never gone to Gokul! We should take him there to have the darshan of Child Krishna, Shri Navanita Priyaji."

Shri Gusainji answered, "Go ahead and try, but Kumbhandas will never cross the Yamuna River, and Gokul is on the other side. Kumbhandas is thoroughly absorbed in the intimate lilas of Shri Nathji on the Govardhan Hill."

One evening they took hold of Kumbhandas' hand and began to talk about the divine moods of Krishna's lilas. They led Kumbhandas down the Govardhan Hill to Anyor and on towards Gokul. Kumbhandas immediately became absorbed in the nectar of devotion and lost all awareness of where he was. All night they praised the divine pastimes. At sunrise, they reached the banks of the Yamuna River across from Gokul. Kumbhandas regained outer awareness, having been absorbed in the nectarous lilas of the Lord, and realized that morning had dawned. He turned and ran as fast as he could back towards Shri Nathji and the Govardhan Hill, thinking, "Who will sing to Shri Nathji this morning? I have lost my Shri Nathji seva!"

When Kumbhandas arrived back at Shri Nathji's temple, he found that Shri Nathji had not yet awoken, though it was two hours later than usual. Shri Gusainji explained, "Shri Nathji Himself has orchestrated this, all for his bhakta Kumbhandas."

Kumbhandas was overjoyed and mused, "I did not miss my singing seva for Shri Nathji!"

One day, Kumbhandas was playing with Shri Nathji in the fields when it came time for the temple darshan to open. As Kumbhandas got up to leave, Shri Nathji asked him, "Where are you going?"

Kumbhandas replied, "I am going to the temple to have Your darshan."

Shri Nathji then objected, "Why would you go there when I am playing right here in front of you?"

Kumbhandas explained, "At the moment, through Your grace, You are here playing with me, but if You suddenly decide to run away, I couldn't stop You. In the temple, however, You were established by Shri Mahaprabhu Vallabhacharya, and You can't leave. You give darshan to everyone there. It is actually because I am so attached to seeing You in Your temple that You now grace me by coming to my home. Through the intensity of Your temple darshan and my kirtan seva there, You bless me by personally appearing to me here. That is why it is essential for me to go have Your darshan in the temple."

Once Kumbhandas saw some lovely mangoes and remembered Shri Nathji in his heart, saying, "These fruits are supremely luscious and worthy to be enjoyed only by You, for You alone relish what is of the highest quality. Partake of these wonderful mangoes."

Later, a Rajput man purchased the mangoes and enjoyed them with his Brahmin companion. That night they both dreamt of Shri Nathji, and the next day they went to Shri Nathji's temple, where the Rajput's mind and heart were captured by Shri Nathji. The Rajput bowed humbly before Shri Gusainji and prayed, "I have wandered about uselessly for such a long time. Now accept me and keep me close to your feet."

Shri Gusainji told him, "You are very fortunate. This condition of yours is due to the grace of Kumbhandasji." The Rajput became an enlightened bhakta and a great vessel of grace.

One time just before Shri Gusainji's birthday, Shri Nathji thought to Himself, "Shri Gusainji celebrates My appearance day with all the other bhaktas in this world, so this year I Myself will arrange for Shri Gusainji's birthday party!" On that day, Shri Nathji requested of Kumbhandas, "Sing something in praise of Shri Gusainji's birthday!" Kumbhandas sang,

Today there is a celebration by Shri Vallabh's door.
The Supreme Being has appeared as Shri Gusainji
*   to spread the grace filled path.*
A fortune has arisen for grace filled souls:
*   He uplifts those who rely on no other means.*
Sings Kumbhandas, "Shri Krishna, Shri Vallabhacharya,
*   and his son, Shri Gusainji embody the essence*
*   of all Vedic practice."*

Kumbhandas sang before Shri Nathji for many years, until his body became weak. When it came time to leave his body, he sat by Sankarshana Lake just below Shri Nathji's temple, and Shri Gusainji came to visit him. "Kumbhandas, tell me, what lila are you contemplating?" his guru asked.

Unable to stand, Kumbhandas nodded his head and mentally bowed to Shri Gusainji and sang:

Krishna, Your gaze has swindled my mind....
When You look at me with those lovely eyes,
*   I am overwhelmed, unable to take a single step.*
Sings Kumbhandas, "You can hold up a mountain,
*   so why can't You talk to me?"*

Lastly, Kumbhandas sang,

Amorous Radha is drenched in the mood
*   of intimate love.*
Like a golden vine, she climbs
*   Krishna, Her dark Tamal tree.*
Her love-plays with the Mountain Holder are diverse.
Sings Kumbhandas, "The Mountain Holder's love play is outstanding."

After singing that poem, Kumbhandas left his body and entered the eternal inner Nikunja Lila of Shri Krishna, through a divine door near Anyor. Shri Gusainji eulogized Kumbhandas, "A great bhakta has disappeared. At this time, bhaktas are concealed in this world."

Kumbhandas was such a vessel of Shri Mahaprabhuji's blessings and a great soul that Shri Nathji and Shri Gusainji remained forever delighted with him. His life story is truly unequalled and inexpressible, so there is no way to fully praise him.

KRISHNADAS

When Krishnadas was only five years old, he began attending satsangs, where bhaktas would gather and discuss Shri Krishna's lilas. If his parents did not let him attend the sacred teachings, he would cry and refuse to eat or drink. He later thought, 'I will go to Vraj and visit all the holy places.' When he beheld Shri Nathji, Krishnadas' heart and mind were swindled. Shri Nathji gazed directly at Krishnadas and said to Shri Mahaprabhuji, "Krishnadas has come! He has been separated from Me for so long, and now I am seeing him again."

Shri Mahaprabhuji walked over to Krishnadas and said, "Krishnadas, come!"

Krishnadas prostrated before Shri Mahaprabhuji and requested, "Maharaj! I have come here through your grace. Please give me shelter." Krishnadas praised his guru,

Those who don't know the form of Shri Vallabh
waste their days in useless spiritual practices.
Sings Krishnadas, "Whoever receives the supreme reward
of his grace filled glance will never be born again."

Shri Vallabhacharya appointed Krishnadas as manager of Shri Nathji's temple. Many years later, after Shri Nathji expressed His wish to the great bhakta Avadhutadas, Krishnadas accordingly removed the Bengali temple priests from Shri Nathji's seva and established Brahmins from Gujarat instead. During Krishnadas' management, Shri Gusainji expanded Shri Nathji's seva with opulent offerings and ornamentation. Tailors, goldsmiths and other craftsmen came to serve in the temple, and Shri Gusainji arranged for all of them to receive a certain ration of Shri Nathji's prasad daily.

When Shri Gusainji came to the temple, he would adorn Shri Nathji and quietly attend to His seva. If anyone asked him something, Shri Gusainji would say, "Go ask Krishnadas. I don't know anything about those matters." Krishnadas' influence and command thereby increased. Wherever Krishnadas went, he rode a chariot and was accompanied by horses, bulls, camels and wagons, and fifty men. He became famous throughout the land. Krishnadas also composed new songs daily and sung them in front of Shri Nathji. He was a great bhakta and recipient of divine grace.

One day, Shri Nathji told Krishnadas, "Tonight, after My evening Arati and seva are completed, bring Shyamkumhar with his drum and come to Parasoli by the Moon Lake. There, I will dance the Rasa Lila." It was a divine evening on the full moon night of the spring month of Chaitra. The lovely beams of the Vraj moon illuminated the scene, and beautiful flowers blossomed on all the vines. While Shri Nathji and Shri Swaminiji danced, Krishnadas sang,

Radha, Brishabhana's daughter,
*   dances with Krishna, the Mountain Holder.*

Their bodies flow as the loving mood
of the Rasa Lila dance builds....
Radha sings in the Maalava raga,
skillfully controlling the beat.
With His beloved at His side, Shri Krishna,
the Lord of beauty, plays the flute....
Krishna is the Moon,
and the Gopis have become the stars,
as they converge in the Rasa Dance circle.

One day, Surdas told Krishnadas, "All of the poems you have composed are but shadows of my own."

"Now I will create a poem that does not resemble any of yours," retorted Krishnadas. Krishnadas sat for three hours, lost in thought, but found that Surdas had already composed a poem about every single lila which came to his mind. Eventually he became discouraged, set his pen and paper down, and went to take his meals. Meanwhile, Shri Nathji arrived and wrote the following line on Krishnadas' paper:

Krishna is coming back from the forest,
accompanied by His cowlads.
His curly locks are covered
with the dust of the Nachuki cows.

The *nachuki* cows which Shri Nathji mentioned in this poem are cows which have given birth for the first time. As they are particularly attentive towards their newborn calves and always hover around them, the cowlads leave the nachuki cows in the cowpen instead of herding them in the forest with the other cows. In this poem, Krishna is returning from the forest, surrounded by an entire herd of nachuki cows, and His curly locks are covered with the dust that has risen from their hooves. Surdas had of course never described such an improbable scene.

When he heard the poem, Surdas replied, "It is true that I have never sung about *nachuki* cows, but Shri Nathji gave you the first line of that poem. I challenged you in a poetry contest, not your Lord!"

Another time Krishnadas was in Agra when he noticed a prostitute teaching her beautiful twelve year old girl how to dance. He became enchanted with her and considered, "This is absolutely supreme! She is a divine soul and fit for Shri Nathji to accept." He brought the young girl and her musical troupe back to Shri Nathji's temple, where he taught her to sing one of his poems, *"My heart is stuck to Krishna's beauty....Krishnadas offers his body, world, and head to the Lord."*

He then brought the girl before Shri Nathji and had her perform before the Blessed Lord. When she sang that last line of the poem, she left her body right there in the temple and attained a divine form in Shri Krishna's Lila.

Another time when a group of bhaktas asked about the ways of the Path of Grace, Krishnadas sang for them,

Speak, 'Krishna, Shri Krishna is my refuge.'
Day and night, daily, every moment, every hour, repeat it....
It invokes constant love for the Lord of Vraj.
Then, without effort you can cross
the fathomless worldly ocean.

Krishnadas had great loving affection towards a woman named Gangabai Kshatrani. Once, while Shri Gusainji was serving Shri Nathji lunch, Gangabai happened to glance at the offerings, so Shri Nathji did not accept them. This precipitated a series of events which actually had their true beginnings in the Lila. In the end Krishnadas became irritated with Shri Gusainji and banned him from Shri Nathji's temple! Shri Gusainji bowed to Shri Nathji's flag and, recalling the Lila incident which led to all this, proceeded to Parasoli by the Moon Lake. He remained there and began to experience divine separation from Shri Nathji, gazing towards Shri Nathji's temple. When Krishnadas noticed Shri Nathji standing by the window looking towards Shri Gusainji, he even had the window sealed!

Shri Gusainji daily wrote a note for his Lord and hid it inside a flower garland which was sent to Shri Nathji. After reading Shri Gusainji's letters, Shri Nathji Himself replied by writing on a betel leaf, using His chewed betel as ink. After reading it, Shri Gusainji would eat the leaf. Shri Gusainji wrote to Shri Nathji, "Lord, without Your sight, Your bhaktas' lives are useless."

Shri Nathji replied, "It is the nature of a cloud to shower rain when the proper time comes....Now persevere, and let the proper time arise. Why suffer such separation?"

Shri Gusainji answered in his next letter, "True, the cloud releases its rain in due time, but without a doubt, the anguished Chataka bird still cries for its water."

Six months later, King Birbal heard about what happened and sent five hundred soldiers to arrest Krishnadas. He then informed Shri Gusainji that he could return to Shri Nathji's temple. Shri Gusainji replied, "I will not eat anything until Krishnadas is released."

When Krishnadas was brought before Shri Gusainji, he humbly touched his guru's feet and sang,

I bow my head to those
who love the dust of the feet
of Shri Vallabh's son.

Shri Gusainji reinstated Krishnadas as the temple manager, at which time Krishnadas again sang,

The son of Vallabh is supremely compassionate.
He blesses his own souls
by placing his hand upon their heads....
Krishnadas praises,
"Everything is accomplished
simply by knowing Shri Gusainji."[2]

Some days later, when Krishnadas went out to inspect a well he was constructing, he slipped and fell into the well. Two men were lowered into the well but emerged without finding his body. Some bhaktas later saw Krishnadas' ghost sitting on top of a tree. When Shri Gusainji heard about Krishnadas' disembodied state, he himself performed the poet's last rites at Dhruva Ghat in Mathura. Only then did Krishnadas drop his ghost form and attain a divine body with which he returned to Shri Krishna's eternal Lila.

Krishnadas was a vessel of Shri Mahaprabhuji's grace. Shri Nathji remains eternally pleased with him, so there is no end to his story. It is beyond description and therefore can never be fully recounted.

NANDADAS

Nandadas was a very well educated Sanodhiya Brahmin and younger brother of the legendary poet Tulsidas.[3] As a young man, Nandadas was very worldly. Tulsidas urged him to settle down and worship Lord Ram. One day, against his

---

[2] Vaishnavas sing this famous poem while waving the arati lights before a descendent of Shri Gusainji (the Vallabhkul Acharyas) who has graced them with a visit to their home.

brother's wishes, Nandadas set out for Dwarka. He lost his way and arrived in Punjab, where he fell in love with another man's wife and vowed, "From today onwards, I will only eat and drink water after I have seen her face." Every day Nandadas sat by the family's door, much to their embarrassment, waiting to see the beautiful woman. Finally the husband and his wife secretly fled town and went to Gokul to visit their guru, Shri Gusainji. Nandadas followed right behind them, and when they reached the Yamuna River, the husband told the boatman, "I will pay you to not take that Brahmin Nandadas to the other side of the River."

When the family reached Gokul and paid their respects to their guru, Shri Gusainji himself arranged plates of prasad for the three of them and one more. When they asked Shri Gusainji who the fourth plate was for, he answered, "The Brahmin who came with you, whom you left on the other side of the river." They became extremely distressed, until Shri Gusainji said, "Why are you troubled? He is a divine soul and has come here due to your association. Now he will no longer trouble you." Shri Gusainji then sent for Nandadas, who was sitting on the banks of Shri Yamuna singing her praises,

O Goddess Yamunaji,
I first came to You because of love.
You understand the condition of Your bhakta's mind.
That is why I have so eagerly run here.
Whatever desires were in my mind and heart
have been fulfilled by worshiping You.

---

[3] Tulsidas is the famous saint-devotee who wrote the Ramachitramanas, a vernacular translation of the epic text Ramayana in praise of Lord Rama. Today, his work is recited throughout India. Tulsidas is considered to be the moon of Hindi literature, while Surdas is referred to as the sun.

Shri Gusainji sent someone to get Nandadas, and when the poet came before Shri Gusainji he prayed, "Maharaj! I have passed my entire life in search of trivial pleasures. You are supremely compassionate; now grace me by taking me under your shelter." After being initiated, Shri Gusainji's divine form became fully established in Nandadas' heart, and he sang the following poem in praise of his guru:

Glories to Shri Gusainji!
You are the light of Shri Vallabh's lineage and
        remover of the world's disturbances.
Glories to you, master of bhaktas, uplifter of the fallen.

Later, as Nandadas partook of the plate of his guru's leftovers, he began to have the direct experience of Krishna's bliss form and lost all bodily awareness. He just sat there, in a state of perfect bliss, for the entire night. The following morning, Shri Gusainji called out to him, "Arise, it is time for darshan." Nandadas bowed to his guru and sang,

When you rise in the morning,
        take the name of Shri Vallabh's son on your tongue....
Nandadas' Lord is the crown jewel of those
        who savor divine mood.
He is my Beloved and reigns
        over the blissful realm of Gokul.

Nandadas proceeded to the temple, where he was delighted by the sight of Shri Navanita Priyaji and began to sing of Shri Krishna's infant Lilas. Later he requested to have the darshan of Shri Nathji. Shri Gusainji took the poet for Shri Nathji's darshan in His temple in Nathdvara, where Nandadas sang,

Shri Nathji's striped, colored turban is so lovely –
how gorgeous are His deer-like eyes!
....Sings Nandadas, "Great is the fortune of those
who behold Hari's face."

Some days later, Tulsidas wrote a letter in which he told Nandadas, "It is improper that you have left the dharma of loyalty to your Husband, Lord Rama."

Nandadas replied, "First I was married to Lord Ram, but in the meantime Shri Krishna came and stole me away. If Lord Ram is so strong, then how could He have let Shri Krishna steal me away? Besides, Lord Ram has only one wife – Shri Sita, so how can He look after a second wife? In fact, He wasn't even able to look after one wife properly, for the demon Ravana abducted her! Shri Krishna, however, is the Lord of infinite women, and after attaining Him as one's Husband, there is no reason to fear. At all times, and without interruption, Krishna affords pleasure to His chosen ones. For this reason, I have made Him my Husband. Please understand this. I have offered my body, mind, and wealth, this world as well as the next, to Shri Krishna. I have fallen under His rule." Nandadas added a poem to his letter:

"Friend, since I heard Krishna's name,
I have become mad and forgotten my home.
My eyes well with tears.
My mind reels, and my voice chokes.
What has happened to my body
is yet another matter....
Sings Nandadas,
"This is what happens to one who hears His name.
Just imagine what will happen
if you see His sweet form!"

Tulsidas decided to go to Vraj and personally retrieve his brother, whom he eventually found near the Govardhan Hill. When Tulsidasji too had the darshan of Shri Nathji but did not bow his head, Nandadas requested Shri Nathji in song, "Tulsidas will only bow his head if You hold Ram's bow and arrow in Your hand."

Hearing Nandadas' prayer, Shri Nathji considered, "Shri Gusainji's disciple is making a request, so I should honor it." Shri Nathji then took the form of Lord Ram [holding a bow and arrow] and gave Tulsidasji His darshan. Tulsidas then fully prostrated himself upon the temple floor.

In Gokul, Tulsidas met Shri Gusainji's fifth son, Shri Raghunathji [one of the names of Shri Ram]. Shri Gusainji called out to his son, "Shri Ramachandraji! One of your followers has come here. Give him your darshan." Raghunathji and his wife, Shri Janaki [the name of Ram's divine consort, Sita], then divinely appeared to Tulsidas as Shri Sita and Lord Ram. Delighted by this darshan of the divine couple, Tulsidas fully prostrated before them and sang,

Now I praise both the towns of Gokul and Ayodhya.
There reside Janaki and her Husband Ram
*   and here, Shyama and Shyam....*
For the benefit of Their bhaktas,
*   Ram and Krishna incarnated as men.*
Tulsidas' hopes lie with them both:
*   They will transport anyone*
*   to the shores of liberation.*

Once Nandadas thought, "My brother Tulsidas has written the story of Lord Ram, the *Ramayana*, in the vernacular. Likewise, I should compose the *Shrimad*

Bhagavatam, depicting the lilas of Lord Krishna, in the local language of Vrajbhasha."

After Nandadas finished writing his version of the tenth canto of the Bhagavat, the Brahmin pundits from Mathura went to Shri Gusainji and complained, "Maharaj! We make our living by reciting the Shrimad Bhagavatam. Now that your disciple, Nandadas has composed it in Vrajbhasha, no one will listen to our discourses, and we will lose our livelihood."

Shri Gusainji then told the poet, "Your Vrajbhasha version of the Shrimad Bhagavatam will detract from the Mathura Brahmins' livelihood. Therefore, keep only what you have composed up to the five Rasa Lila chapters, and offer the rest of the text into the Yamuna River." The poet followed his guru's instructions.

Once Emperor Akbar came to Mathura. Among his entourage was a maidservant named Rup Manjari, who was a disciple of Shri Gusainji. Nandadas was deeply in love with Rup Manjari and went to meet with her. He found her in an isolated forest at Bilachu, where she was preparing some food offerings for Shri Nathji. When Shri Nathji appeared there to accept her offerings, Nandadas beheld the Lord and delightedly thought, "Rup Manjari is truly fortunate."

Rup Manjari offered Nandadas some prasad and told him, "I wish I could remain here in Vraj with you forever."

"The Lord will arrange it for you," Nandadas responded.

Meanwhile, the court singer Tansen had sung one of Nandadas' poems before the Emperor, with the line: "Krishna calls out with His flute, 'Shri Radhe! Radhe!' while Nandadas sings close by."

The next day, the Emperor summoned Nandadas and asked him, "How could you have come anywhere near the Rasa Lila dance?"

Nandadas replied, "You would not believe me if I told you. But there is one maidservant named Rup Manjari in your entourage. Ask her about it; she knows."

The Emperor asked Rup Manjari, "What is the meaning of Nandadas' poem about the Rasa Lila?" Hearing the Emperor's words, she immediately fell to the ground and left her material body. She attained entrance into Shri Krishna's eternal Lila realm. Emperor Akbar ran back to Nandadas and to his great astonishment found that Nandadas too had left his body and returned to Krishna's eternal Lila. The bewildered Emperor asked Raja Birbal, "Why did they both leave their bodies like this?"

Raja Birbal explained, "They kept their dharma secret. Such matters as the Rasa Lila cannot be explained or spoken of. They had no other solution but to leave their material bodies."

Both Nandadas and Rup Manjari were such accomplished souls. Nandadas was truly a vessel of grace and accomplished bhakta. Shri Gusainji was always pleased with him and revealed to the poet the bliss of his divine form. There is no way to fully tell his story.

CHITA SWAMI

Chita Swami was a Chaube Brahmin from Mathura. He was the ringleader of a group of four other Brahmins, all rascals by nature. One day he and his cohorts schemed, "Gusainji in Gokul casts many spells. Whoever goes to see him falls under his sway. Let's go to Gokul and trick Shri Gusainji by offering him a fake coin and an empty coconut."

As Chita Swami gazed upon Shri Gusainji, he suddenly saw Lord Krishna sitting in his place. He felt guilty, "I came to play a joke on Shri Gusainji, but he is *Sakshat Purna Purushottama* – the actual manifestation of the fully divine

supreme Being! How stupid of me to come here to fool him."
He hid the empty coconut and counterfeit coin.

Shri Gusainji warmly greeted him, "Chita Swami, I
have not seen you for a long time. How are you?" After Chita
Swami requested and received initiation, he sang,

Now I have recognized Krishna.
I came here to deceive,
    not knowing the Supreme Lord....
He saw me and made me His own.

Shri Gusainji then said, "You brought a coconut for
me. Why are you hiding it?"

Chita Swami face shriveled as he realized, "Shri
Gusainji is the Lord Himself. If he knows that I brought a
coconut, he must also know that it is hollow!" He submitted,
"Maharaj! You know about all of my deeds. Now forgive me
for what I have done."

"Don't hold any doubts in your mind. Now you are
mine, so what is there to fear? Bring me the coconut."

To Chita Swami's amazement, the coconut was
opened and found to be perfectly ripe. Chita Swami then
sang,

I take the shelter of his lotus-petal like feet.
The son of Shri Vallabh is an ocean of grace.
    He grabbed hold of my arm and delivered me
        from the worldly flow.

That afternoon Shri Gusainji told Chita Swami to go
have Shri Navanita Priyaji's darshan in the temple. As soon
as he entered, Chita Swami saw Shri Gusainji standing there
and thought to himself, "I just left Shri Gusainji in his room.
How did he get here? Perhaps there is another route within

the temple." When he exited the darshan hall, however, he again saw Shri Gusainji in his room, seated upon a cushion. Chita Swami was shocked that Shri Gusainji could appear in two places at once. The next day Shri Gusainji sent the poet to Nathdvara to have Shri Nathji's darshan. There he saw Shri Gusainji standing next to Shri Nathji, but when he asked everyone when Shri Gusainji had arrived, they answered, "Shri Gusainji is not here. He is in Gokul."

When he mentioned the divine event to Shri Gusainji, the guru just smiled. Chita Swami realized that, "Shri Nathji and Shri Gusainji are truly one form." With this insight, he then sang,

Glories to Gopal, Who lived in Gokul
     and has now returned as Shri Gusainji
        to reside once again in His hometown....
Sings Chita Swami,
"Shri Gusainji is Krishna and
     Krishna is Shri Gusainji:
        of this there is no doubt."

Birbal, Chita Swami's religious client and an important minister, later heard that poem and rebuked Chita Swami, "If our Muslim Emperor, Akbar, hears these poems of yours about Shri Gusainji being Shri Krishna, how will you explain yourself?"

Chita Swami replied, "Your mind has become defiled. I will never look at your face again."

When Emperor Akbar heard about the event, he told his minister, "Birbal, what Chita Swami sang is true. I had a magic jewel that yielded two ounces of gold every day, and I gave it to Shri Gusainji. Taking it into his hands, he asked me three times, 'You are giving this to me?' Each time I replied, 'Yes.' Then Shri Gusainji threw it into the Yamuna River! I immediately demanded, 'Give me back my jewel!'

"Shri Gusainji then dipped his hand into the Yamuna River and withdrew a handful of identical jewels. He said to me, 'If your jewel is among these, select it and take it back.'

"When I did not take any of the jewels, he asked me three times, 'You are sure you don't want your jewel back now?'

"After I replied, 'No,' three times, he threw them all back into the Yamuna River. Birbal, you should not have such doubts or speak such things to your religious guide, because Shri Gusainji is indeed the Lord Himself."

Chita Swami was never concerned about money or other worldly issues. He was totally absorbed in singing his guru's praises. When he heard that Shri Gusainji had left this world, Chita Swami fell unconscious to the ground. At that time, Shri Nathji appeared to him and said, "Until now, I have appeared to you in two forms: as Krishna and as Shri Gusainji. Now I will let you experience Me in Shri Gusainji's seven sons." Chita Swami then beheld their divinity and sang,

Krishna has taken on seven forms
and now plays as Shri Gusainji's seven sons....
Shri Gusainji is Krishna. By worshipping Him,
everything is accomplished."

Chita Swami was a vessel of Shri Gusainji's grace and an intimate bhakta. To what extent can we praise his story?

GOVINDA SWAMI

Govinda Swami had many disciples and was a great poet and musician. One day he met a follower of Shri Gusainji and asked him, "How is it possible to directly know Shri Krishna's lilas?"

When Chita Swami persisted, the Vaishnava finally told him that "through Shri Gusainji, one can attain the lotus feet of the Lord." Chita Swami insisted on going to Gokul right away. In Gokul he saw Shri Gusainji performing his sandhya prayers, and Govinda Swami thought, "This guru is some great karma yogi who performs Vedic rituals. How could he possibly unite anyone with Shri Krishna?"

Just then Shri Gusainji called out to him, "Govinda Das! When did you come?"

Govinda Swami thought, "How did he know my name?"

After having the darshan of Shri Navanita Priyaji in Shri Gusainji's home, Chita Swami remarked, "Maharaj! You are very tricky. On the outside it appears that you are just performing Vedic rites, but Shri Krishna Himself actually resides here in your home!"

The guru replied, "The path of devotion is a flower, and the path of karma is like the thorns."

Shri Harirayaji would later illuminate this teaching by explaining that, "Without the thorns of proper action, the devotional flower cannot bloom and will not remain. Devotion is a secret thing and therefore should not be openly exposed."

After Govinda Swami became Shri Gusainji's disciple, he began to have direct experience with Shri Krishna. One day, Shri Gusainji asked Govinda Swami, "How does Krishna sing?"

"Krishna sings well," replied Govinda Swami, "but His consort, Shri Swaminiji, has an even more melodious voice. To hear Her sing with Krishna is truly an experience." Hearing his reply, Shri Gusainji laughed.

Once a group of bhaktas from Govinda Swami's town came looking for him to become his disciples. They asked around for Govinda Swami and eventually found his house, where his sister, Kanhabai told them, "He went to bathe near Yashoda Ghat."

Not recognizing the poet when they happened upon him by the Yamuna River, they asked him, "Where is Govinda Swami?"

He replied, "Govinda Swami died many days ago."

They returned disappointed to Govindadas' house. When Govindadas arrived there a short while later, they recognized him and protested, "You told us that Govinda Swami had died, but you are him! Swami, why did you tell us that you had died?"

"If he hasn't died yet," replied Govinda Das, "now he will."

In this way Govinda Swami revealed that he was no longer a Swami, but a follower, Govinda 'Das.'

Govindadas never bathed in the Yamuna River; he would not so much as place his feet in her sacred waters. Instead, he would roll in her sands and sip her water. Knowing the Yamuna River to be the physical form of Krishna's divine consort, Shri Yamunaji, he thought, "How can I put this useless body into her sacred waters?" Govindadas was filled with the deepest bhava for Shri Yamunaji's divine form.

Govindadas imbibed the teachings of Shri Gusainji deeply into his heart was a full recipient of his guru's grace. Shri Nathji used to play with him.

Once, while Govindadas was standing in the temple singing kirtan, Shri Nathji suddenly threw some pebbles which struck Govindadas in the back. After Shri Nathji threw pebbles at him a second and third time, Govindadas threw a pebble back at Shri Nathji, which startled Him. Shri Gusainji reprimanded the poet, "Govindadas! What did you just do?"

"Do you only think about your own Son?" replied Govindadas. "He threw three stones at me. Just look at my back!" Govindadas showed Shri Gusainji where the stones had struck him on the back, and added, "After all, in play, no one is a big shot!"

Once during the Holi season, Govinda Swami suddenly stopped singing in the middle of a poem. Shri Gusainji questioned, "Govindadas! Why have you stopped singing?"

"Maharaj," Govindadas replied, "I just sang, 'Krishna stealthily sneaks up behind the Gopis, smears their cheeks, and dashes away.' Krishna dashed away, and my heart and mind went with Him. Since He ran away, how can there be any more play?" Shri Gusainji was enthralled to hear the poet's reply.

During the winter, Shri Nathji and Govindadas used to play in a grove of Kadamba trees called Shyam Dak. One day, Shri Nathji was sitting up in a tree while His cows grazed all around in the forest. Meanwhile, Shri Gusainji entered Shri Nathji's temple back in Nathdvara. At that moment, Shri Nathji told Govindadas, "I must return to My temple! It is time for the afternoon seva to begin. What will Shri Gusainji say if he doesn't find Me in the temple?" As Shri Nathji quickly scrambled down the tree and rushed back to the temple, one of His garments got caught on a branch and ripped.

Just as Shri Nathji arrived in the temple and took His seat, Shri Gusainji opened the doors for the afternoon Utthapan darshan and saw His torn cloth. Shri Gusainji was forlorn, "One of Shri Nathji's garments is ripped. I don't know what dishonor has caused this to happen."

Govindadas laughed and said, "Maharaj! Don't you know the nature of your Boy? When you were about to enter the temple this afternoon, He scurried down from the top of a tree, and His cloth caught on a branch and ripped."

Shri Gusainji considered for some time and then told all the temple staff, "From now on, blow the conch three times and then wait a moment before opening the temple doors. This will allow Shri Nathji enough time to return to His temple."

Shri Nathji used to make Govindadas act like a horse and carry him around the forest on his back. One day, a Vaishnava saw Govindadas standing in the middle of the road urinating. Shri Gusainji questioned Govindadas, "What is this Vaishnava saying? You were standing in the road peeing?"

Govindadas replied, "Do horses ever sit to urinate? How could I have stopped to squat down and pee while I was carrying Shri Nathji? That Vaishnava saw me, but he didn't see Shri Nathji saddled on my back."

Once another bhakta complained to Shri Gusainji that Govindadas took his lunch early, before Rajbhog Arati. When Shri Gusainji questioned Govindadas, the poet replied, "As soon as the seva is completed and the Rajbhog Arati lights have been waved, your Boy Shri Nathji comes to me and says, 'Govindadas! Let's go play!' That's why I take prasad before everyone else."

"One shouldn't take prasad before Rajbhog," Shri Gusainji insisted. "Come take prasad after Rajbhog Arati."

The following day, Govindadas sat down with everyone else after Rajbhog Arati to take his meal. Meanwhile, Shri Nathji came out of the inner temple looking for him. When he finally arrived, Shri Nathji questioned, "What took you so long? I have come here three times looking for you."

That afternoon Shri Nathji told Shri Gusainji, "You ordered Govindadas to eat after Rajbhog Arati, so today I was delayed from going out to play in the forest. Tell Govindadas that he should take his lunch early, like he did before."

Shri Gusainji happily told the poet, "Govindadas! Take your lunch as you did before. There is no fault in your doing so." Govindadas was such a vessel of Shri Nathji's grace, a great bhakta and intimate friend of the Lord.

One summer day, Govindadas accompanied Shri Gusainji to a Krishna temple in Mathura. When he saw Shri Keshoraya (a form of Krishna) adorned in very heavy cloth and jewels, despite the season and weather, Govindadas asked the deity, "Maharaj! Are You alright?"

Shri Gusainji heard Govindadas' comment and turned to look at him with a grin, but while leaving the temple, he said, "Govindadas, you should not say things like that."

"It is such a hot day," Govindadas replied, "yet Shri Keshorayaji was covered with gold and silver laced *jari* cloth below, above, and all around. What else can I say?" Shri Gusainji silently smiled.

Govindadas sang kirtan on a hill in the town of Mahavan. Shri Gusainji's fourth son, Shri Gokulnathji came to listen daily, because he was such a great singer. As Shri Gusainji was about to leave his body, he took Govindadas by the arm, and they walked together into a cave on the Govardhan Hill, at the Sundar Shila in Nathdvara (now Jatipura). They both entered into Krishna's eternal Lila with their material bodies. Govindadas was such a vessel of Shri Gusainji's grace and intimate bhakta of the Lord.

CHATURBHUJADAS

Chaturbhujadas was born in the town of Yamunavata as the sixth son of the poet bhakta Kumbhandas. Before Chaturbhujadas was born, his father was distressed that his first five sons were so attached to worldly ways. He regretted, "I don't have a single son with whom I can share my heart."

One day, Shri Nathji asked him, "Kumbhana, why are you so sad?"

"Maharaj," Kumbhandas replied, "I don't have any satsang!"

Shri Nathji smiled and said, "I am the fruit of all satsang, and I chase after you! Yet still you desire good association?"

Kumbhandas replied, "None other than the great bhaktas can fathom the ecstasy that resides within Your form, so without their association, one's heart cannot fully adhere to You."

Shri Nathji laughed and exclaimed, "Kumbhana! You are blessed. I will grant you a great devotional soul for a son with whom you can have satsang."

One day Shri Nathji appeared to Kumbhandas and said, "Come with Me!" They went to the home of a Gopi dairymaid who had stored her curds and butter in clay pots and hung them up high before going out to do some other work. Shri Nathji began to take curds from the jug with His hands. When His shawl suddenly came loose and fell to the ground, He manifested two additional lower arms with which to pick up the shawl. Kumbhandas thus had the darshan of Lord Krishna in His *Chaturbhuja* (four-armed) form.

Just then, the Gopi returned home and began to chase after Shri Nathji, trying to grab hold of Him. Shri Nathji spit a mouthful of milk right in her face, and while her eyes were drenched with milk, Kumbhandas and Shri Nathji escaped. Kumbhandas sang of this incident,

This time she really caught Hari,
stealing and eating her curds and butter,
as He daily does.
The pretty Vraj maiden blocked the door;
the sound of her anklet bells startled Him....

Kumbhandas' Lord is trapped
    by that Gopi's loving mood.
He fills His mouth with milk,
    spits it into her eyes,
        and scrambles away.

When his wife gave birth to their son that very day, Kumbhandas decided, "I will call him Chaturbhujadas: follower of the four-armed Lord."

Shri Gusainji blessed him, "Your newborn son will give you great happiness. The wish of your heart has been fulfilled." At the time of infant Chaturbhujadas' initiation from Shri Gusainji, he experienced all of Shri Krishna's lilas, and the divine form of Shri Gusainji became firmly established in his heart. Then infant Chaturbhujadas sang:

Shri Gusainji, the son of Vallabhacharya
    is the source of all pleasures for his followers.
My heart is filled with joy just by seeing Him....
Sings Chaturbhujadas, "Shri Gusainji uplifts the fallen.
    His grace is all-encompassing."

From the day he received initiation, Chaturbhujadas would not even drink milk until he had seen Shri Nathji! Whenever they were all alone, infant Chaturbhujadas would begin to speak to his father about the divine lilas and bhavas of Shri Nathji, Shri Mahaprabhuji and Shri Gusainji. They both were filled with bliss from these discussions. If someone else came nearby, Chaturbhujadas would again act like an innocent infant.

When Chaturbhujadas was a young boy, Shri Nathji used to take him out in the forest with His cows and cowlad friends and to steal curds from the dairymaids' homes. One night, while Kumbhandas and Chaturbhujadas were sitting together at home, they saw lights shimmering in the distance in Shri Nathji's temple. Kumbhandas then sang to his son,

Look at the light in the window!
There Hari rests in a lofty room
*   filled with love paintings.*

Chaturbhujadas then continued:

Beloved Krishna is making great efforts
*   to behold His beloved's lovely face.*

Kumbhandas was very happy to hear his son's words. Then, full of divine mood, he completed the poem,

He thrills Her by placing His arm around Her neck.
*   Now, She drinks the nectar of His lips.*
Her body, mind and heart merge with the love of Her life,
*   while Her fresh form overflows with beauty.*
Sings Kumbhandas, "Krishna's fortune has climaxed.
*   The Couple have joined into a single essence:*
Youthful, enchanting, wise Radha
*   and forever novel Mountain-Holder Krishna."*

Chaturbhujadas also sang poems before Shri Nathji in the temple:

My friend! Today, tomorrow, and every day,
*   He is always more and more.*
Behold nectar-filled Krishna!
....Chaturbhujadas imbibes His nectar form
*   and remains forever in His shelter.*

Once, a 'Rasa Lila' dance performance group came to Parasoli by the Moon Lake. The group began the dance mandala in the early evening, and after they had danced for almost the entire night, Shri Gokulnathji told Chaturbhujadas, "Now you sing something."

"I will only sing if I see Shri Nathji Himself comes here and dances the Rasa," Chaturbhujadas replied. Soon thereafter, Shri Nathji arrived and began to dance the Rasa Lila with the Gopis of Vraj. The night grew longer and the moon even more luminous, and Chaturbhujadas sang,

Adorned in a fantastic dancer's dress,
    beautiful Mountain Holder Shyam,
    a treasure of virtues, dances the Rasa
        by the banks of the Yamuna River.

One morning Shri Gusainji asked Chaturbhujadas to go out and collect some flowers. Chaturbhujadas eventually came near a cave in the Govardhan Hill. Suddenly, he beheld Shri Nathji and Shri Swaminiji, Who had just arisen and emerged from the cave. While he had this darshan, Chaturbhujadas sang,

Awaking this morning, the Son of Nanda
    and the Darling of Brishabhana
        are drenched in the mood of love....
The garlands on Their chests are withered.
    Their ornaments are in disarray....
Seeing the delight of this Couple,
Chaturbhujadas offers Them
    his body, wealth and heart.

Later, when Chaturbhujadas had grown, Shri Nathji told him, "Chaturbhujadas! Get married." Chaturbhujadas followed Shri Nathji's order and married, but his wife died after only a few days. Chaturbhujadas then entered the customary period of mourning, during which time he was not allowed into Shri Nathji's temple. Afflicted with separation from his beloved Lord, Chaturbhujadas passed the days by sitting in the forest singing kirtans like these:

I love to see Krishna in the morning.
It is the supreme reward of my eyes to behold His •
*   lovely cheeks and attractive, unsteady eyes.*

When he was finally able to return to the temple, Shri Nathji called out to him, "Chaturbhujadas! Now get married again!" Immediately following the second marriage, Shri Nathji began to joke with his friends, "Kumbhandas' son got married, and after his wife died, he only waited a few months before immediately getting married again! And still he is not satisfied!"

One day Chaturbhujadas told Shri Nathji off, "You make fun of me like this every day, but You run around with women from every house in Vraj!"

Hearing Chaturbhujadas' words, Shri Nathji became embarrassed and stopped speaking to him. He later went to Shri Gusainji and said, "Tell Chaturbhujadas never to speak to Me like that again."

Chaturbhujadas defended himself, "Shri Nathji makes fun of me every day, so one time I also let Him have it."

Shri Gusainji rebuked him, "From now on, never speak to the Beloved Lord like that again."

From that day, even if Shri Nathji teased Chaturbhujadas, he would say nothing in return. Shri Nathji continued to joke like that, bestowing His grace upon Chaturbhujadas and giving the poet direct experience of Himself.

Once when Shri Girdharji took Shri Nathji to Mathura, Chaturbhujadas felt great separation from the Lord and sang,

To whom can I speak of
the agony of my attachment?
....Without Your sight, my eyes flitter
like a fish out of water,
and every blink of an eye seems like an age.
O Krishna, lovely Lad of the Govardhan Hill –
I cannot remain without You.

After singing such poems in extreme separation, Chaturbhujadas heard the jingling bells of cows and then saw Krishna and His brother Balaram approaching, surrounded by Their cowlad friends. "I will return to My temple tomorrow," Shri Nathji assured him.

Shri Gusainji later commented, "Shri Nathji is very kind and cannot bear the distress of His bhaktas."

Shri Gokulnathji once invited Chaturbhujadas to accompany him to Gokul. Beholding Shri Krishna's child form, the poet sang,

I rejoice over You, Navanita Priya,
Infant Krishna who loves fresh butter....
Watching You, my eyes are totally satisfied.
O dark and lovely one, You are the breath
and wealth of my life.

When Chaturbhujadas returned and told his father where he had been, Kumbhandas said, "You have fallen from grace to law." Shri Gusainji overheard the remark from inside the temple and laughed.

Later Shri Gusainji explained, "Kumbhandas' heart is stuck on Shri Nathji and cannot endure one second of separation from Him. For that reason, he considers all of Krishna's other lilas to be restricted by law. Actually, Krishna's infant lilas and adolescent lilas are one." From that day, Chaturbhujadas never left the Govardhan Hill to go anywhere else.

When Chaturbhujadas heard that Shri Gusainji had entered a cave on the Govardhan Hill with his body, he fell down to the ground in profound separation and sang,

Shri Vitthalesh, please reside here in Vraj again!
With your grace, give me your sight once more –
in that lila, and in that dress.
Make the path of devotion arise again!

Then, knowing of Chaturbhujadas' extreme separation, Shri Gusainji appeared in a supremely blissful form within the poet's heart and said, "Chaturbhujadas, why are you so distressed? I am always with you! Therefore, don't be so saddened in your mind. From now on, see me close to Shri Nathji. Know that I am always close to Shri Govardhan Nathji, for that is where I remain."

No one has ever been, nor will ever be
equal to Lord Shri Gusainji.
Such splendor was unheard of before and
will never be seen again,
for it just is not possible to recreate....
Who will be such a pillar of dharma,
replete with knowledge and action,
and again reveal devotion in this world?
Chaturbhujadas prays,
"Let Shri Gusainji's remembrance
be the crown of my life."

While singing many such poems in praise of his guru,
Chaturbhujadas fixed his mind and heart upon Shri
Gusainji's lotus feet. He then left his material body, and he
too entered Shri Krishna's eternal Lila. Chaturbhujadas was
a vessel of Shri Gusainji's grace and a great bhakta. There is
no way to fully tell his story.

7.
SEVA

Shri Krishna, dark as a rain-filled cloud, adorned with peacock feathers, wild flowers and a gunja bead necklace, graces the banks of the Yamuna River. When He applies His lips to the flute, melodious notes fill Vrindavan and enrapture the hearts of the love-smitten dairymaids, the Gopis. This Krishna, a herder of cows, the son of Yashoda, the butter-thief and the beloved of the Gopis, is the object, means and reward of the grace filled practice of seva, Shri Krishna's pleasing worship.

Shri Vallabhacharya explained that to attain the Lord, you must please Him. True seva arises when the mind and heart are threaded into the blessed practice of worshipping Shri Krishna. In order to attain this state, bhaktas employ their bodies and their wealth in His seva. Shri Krishna Himself established the foundations of the Path of Grace on the auspicious 11th night in the bright half of the month of Shravan. At midnight, the blessed Lord appeared before Shri Vallabhacharya by the banks of the Yamuna River in Gokul and gave him the Brahma Sambandha mantra, with instructions to initiate bhaktas with that sacred formula. It constitutes a spiritual marriage, connecting the soul to its divine source. This Sanskrit mantra is to this day given to Pushti initiates by a descendant of Shri Vallabhacharya's lineage.

After this initiation, the bhakta is eligible to perform Shri Krishna's seva. Seva is an integral part of Shri Vallabh's doctrine. It uses flowers, fruits and other materials found in this world for His pleasure. It is performed within the bhakta's own world, in the home. When seva is infused with bhava, divine inspiration, a Lila realm arises in the material sphere. When seva matures, it fills the heart with His joy and continues effortlessly. Seva is motivated by love. It is considered to be the main dharma of grace filled souls. Shri Vallabhacharya tells us, "One should always be engaged in Shri Krishna's seva."[34]

Seva can be offered to Shri Krishna in any divine mood which arises within the bhakta, be it the tender parental mood of mother Yashoda or the passion of the Gopis. In any case, it always begins with the feeling that "I am Shri Krishna's *Das* – His devoted follower." The full nine-fold devotion revealed by the bhakta Prahlad is contained within the loving acts of seva: the sevak remembers Krishna's lilas (*smaranam*), sings His praises (*kirtanam*), listens to His glories (*shravanam*), bows to Him (*vandanam*) and reverently touches His feet (*pada sevanam*). She arranges and cleans a place for Him to reside (*archanam*). Offering all types of worship to the Beloved by collecting the necessary things for His seva, she becomes His true follower (*dasyam*). Through seva, with grace, the bhakta may reach the level of being Shri Krishna's friend (*sakhyam*), and ultimately offers her soul and everything to Him in the exalted state of complete soulful offering, called *atma nivedanam*. This total offering is the beginning and the end of seva.

Shri Vallabhacharya identifies devotion as progressing through three stages: love, attachment, and addiction. "*Divine love* removes worldly hankering. When one becomes *attached* to the Beloved, one loses all taste for the worldly home and sees it as unconnected to one's true self. When the bhakta becomes *totally addicted* to Shri Krishna and can no longer live without Him, that blessed one has attained devotional excellence."[35]

Shri Krishna's seva can be found in the traditional homes (called *Havelis*) of Shri Vallabhacharya's descendants as well as in the houses of their followers. In his Shri Subodhini text, Shri Vallabhacharya calls Lord Krishna a "householder." In Vedic tradition, the majority of teachers and sages who have transmitted the paths of enlightenment have been householders. Although Shri Krishna wanders the forest havens of Vrindavan, He actually lives at home and resides with His mother, Yashoda. He is also at home with His bhaktas and makes special visits to the houses of His beloved Gopis, the dairymaids of Vraj.

Shri Krishna's householder tradition has been continued by Shri Vallabhacharya and his descendants. The lineage holders' Havelis, found throughout India, have housed the various forms and lilas of Shri Krishna since the times of Shri Vallabhacharya. The sacred architecture of the Haveli always centers around Shri Krishna's pleasure and His blessed worship. His inner temple sanctuary is the most private part of the house. The kitchens are also hidden away from onlookers. A porch with triple archways, called the Dol Tivari provides a space for Shri Krishna to swing during the spring and rainy seasons. A large courtyard, considered to be the formless aspect of the Supreme Brahman, is where bhaktas congregate to have Shri Krishna's darshan.

Traditionally, followers would come to pay their respects to their guru in his Haveli. While there, they would take the blessed opportunity to have darshan of the guru's personal Krishna seva. To see Shri Krishna at home with the Vallabh lineage holders inspires bhaktas to make Shri Krishna's seva in their own homes. Wherever Shri Krishna resides is Vrindavan, and the bhakta's natural dharma is to worship Shri Krishna at home.

Shri Vallabhacharya developed the initial forms of seva, and his son, Shri Gusainji further revealed the practice.

Shri Gusainji was an enlightened poet and musician as well as a creative artist who devoted his manifold talents in Shri Krishna's seva. He gifted us with the elaborate modes of grace filled worship. Seva is a continuing process and develops in unique ways, according to the temperaments of the bhaktas. The stories of the followers of Shri Vallabhacharya and Shri Gusainji (the 84 and 252 Vaishnava vartas) reveal to us some of the ways seva has been performed.

Shri Krishna's seva is very personal. It differs from the practice of puja because it is driven not by mantra, but by love. Although it has a format, the main concern is His pleasure. In a condition of grace, the rules can be transcended if it is for His delight. Shri Vallabhacharya identified the fruits of performing seva:

"From the moment the Blessed Lord gives the divine reward of His Presence, the bhakta's spiritual desires are fulfilled. Time is never a controlling factor regarding eligibility and the three rewards of seva. These rewards are the capacity to experience transcendent love, to be absorbed into Krishna's Lila, and to attain a spiritual form that is useful in eternal realms. Anxiety, obstructions, and worldly enjoyment are the three things that hinder seva." [36]

The blessed Lord made this world, and so it is fit for His pleasure. Fresh flowers, vegetables, grains, fruits, dry fruits and water are all offered to Shri Krishna. He promises in the Bhagavat Gita that however His bhaktas worship Him, so He honors them in return and accepts whatever is offered with love. The practice of seva is open to anyone who feels the rush of His presence. Lord Krishna's seva as performed in Shri Nathji's temple and the lineage holders' Havelis is eight-fold, revolving around Shri Krishna's daily life. Shri Krishna lives with and for His bhaktas, and they honor Him from the moment He rises in the morning until He retires for the evening.

The object of seva is always the multi-dimensional Shri Krishna. While infant Krishna swings in mother Yashoda's cradle, He relates to the Gopis as their Lover. Shri Krishna appears for the bhaktas' benefit, to accept their various types of seva. He also limits Himself in order to please His beloveds. His grace filled concealment allows His bhaktas to discover Him within their own homes. Unlimited Divinity is unapproachable, and so His bhaktas limit Him – all with His grace. For them, He is not the Lord of the universe, but a Child who will dance for a glass of buttermilk, as described by Rasakhan, the legendary poet and disciple of Shri Gusainji:

The gods Shesh, Ganesh, Mahesh,
*   Suresh and Dinesh constantly sing of Him*
Who is beginningless, endless, unlimited, indestructible,
*   void of differences, and revealed in the Vedas.*
Narada, Sukha, and Vyasa are exhausted from searching for Him.
*   They can never fathom His limits.*
Yet, the dairymaids of Vrindavan can make Him dance –
*   for a sip of buttermilk from the palm of their hands!*

Krishna seva is a joyous and beautiful affair. A multitude of arts are employed in His pleasing seva. Everything is dedicated to Him and becomes sanctified after He enjoys it. Shri Krishna is served food (*bhog*) in astounding varieties, always prepared with the finest ingredients. He is adorned with a variety of the finest clothes and jewelry (*shringar*), sensitive to the season and festival. Seva is also replete with music (*raga*). Poems composed by the great bhaktas are sung in ragas and rhythms which correspond to the various seasons, festivals and times of day. Everything is offered to Shri Krishna, the Master of enjoyment.

Many bhaktas have a svarupa, a form of Shri Krishna, which resides with them in their homes. Shri Krishna's seva can be made in the form of a hand-painted picture, a three-dimensional svarupa made of wood, black marble, or metal, or even sacred sands, cloth and texts. Svarupas are often handed down from generation to generation. They are regarded and worshiped as Shri Krishna Himself. Food offerings are offered and become *prasad*, portions of grace.

In many homes of worship, Shri Krishna is accompanied by Shri Swaminiji (Shri Radha). By replicating the daily routine of Krishna's activities, bhaktas transform their homes into Krishna's own. Their town becomes Krishna's town of Gokul. Shri Krishna fulfills for them each of the traditional four pursuits of life: *dharma, artha, kama*, and *moksha*. His worship is their dharma, and their wealth is Shri Krishna Himself. Their desires are fulfilled when He resides in their hearts, and to always serve and remember Him is liberation.[37]

Shri Vallabhacharya's descendants serve Shri Krishna at eight different times during the day beginning early in the morning. After lunch there is a four hour break before the afternoon and evening worship. During eight darshans, the temple doors are briefly opened for the bhaktas to have the auspicious sight of Shri Krishna. Each darshan has its own time, mood, and lila. Not all darshans are always open to the public, and some lineage holders do not allow the public darshan at all.

The seva performed in the homes of the bhaktas follows a similar format but rarely includes eight separate darshans. Home worship is done according to the ability of the bhakta. The gurus of the path of seva are the Gopis, who worshipped Shri Krishna as their Beloved, while Mother Yashoda is the role model for worshipping Shri Krishna as a Child. These two moods can mingle, but they both arise from the foundations of devotional servitude. The bhakta poet Surdas sings about the practice of daily seva:

"Those who have surrendered their bodies to the Blessed Lord offer Him only the best things. Those who bring the Lord a jug of water hold a position in the eternal realms. Those who clean the temple are never caught in the Lord's maya. Those who clean the Lord's grains receive the fruit of visiting all the sacred shrines. Those who make the Lord a garland entertain a great devotee daily. Those who bring sandal-paste for the Lord are relieved of life's threefold miseries. Those who clean the Lord's vessels remain forever pure. Those who blissfully sing of the Lord's glories attain all four types of liberation."

Mangala

Shri Krishna's daily seva begins early in the morning, when He is awoken with the ringing of a bell and sound of the conch, and then immediately offered a seasonal and sumptuous breakfast of sweets, milk, curd, butter, etc.

Krishna's Awakening
Raga Bhairav

O, Lalana: Awake; it is morning!
Enjoy this milk, curds, sweets,
*   and a roti bread with butter.*
Lotuses are blooming; everyone is singing,
*   their voices so pure.*
Everywhere birds are chirping.
Sings Rasika Pritam,
"Yashoda bids her Beloved Krishna,
*   'Now get up - Nanda Kishor!'"*

After breakfast, the temple doors are opened for darshan and the Mangala Arati lights are waved. The following poem by Shri Gusainji is sung every day:

Raga Bhairav

Auspicious, auspicious is the morning.
Auspicious are Nanda and Yashoda
    as they sing splendid songs and lovingly care
        for their Krishna, who sits in their laps.
Shri Krishna is the essence of the Vedas.
The auspicious sound of His name
    eradicates the pains of His distressed bhaktas.
The feelings of the Gopis, Krishna's friends, the cows and deer
    create an auspicious treasure of nectar beyond description.
Auspicious is Krishna's gentle smile.
    as He gazes and speaks.
His nose points upward while
    His pearl nose-ring quivers.
His soft fingertips move over the flute's holes,
    creating melodies that enchant all of Vrindavan.
Auspicious are all the Gopis.
They are enraptured and bewildered
    by the melody of the Rasa dance,
        and now move with languid gait.
Eternal victory to You, Holder of the Mountain!
    You shelter Your intimate followers.

Raga Bhairav

O, friend, come and see Gopal's morning arati!
Every morning I am so blessed to discover Krishna's face
    and behold His wide eyes.
The beautiful Shyam is so auspicious.

His lovely forehead contains
those favorable eyebrows.
Sings Chaturbhujadas,
"Mountain-Holder Krishna is forever
my auspicious treasure."

Shringaar

After Mangala, Shri Krishna is bathed and adorned with garments and jewelry appropriate for the season. After the ornamentation is complete, a mirror is held up for Shri Krishna to behold Himself; He sits surrounded by soft cushions, with paintings or other types of wall hangings decorating His inner temple chambers. Knowing what Krishna enjoys as well as when to offer it is true knowledge in the Path of Grace. With this sensitivity, Shri Krishna comes alive for His bhaktas and relates to them on a personal level.

Ornamentation:
Raga Vilaval

Come, Gopal!
It's time for me to adorn You.
First I anoint You with various scented soaps
and bathe You with warm water.
Now I dry You with a towel, braid Your hair,
and lovingly make You a flower garland.
On Your head I tie a red turban adorned with jewels
and top it with a silver plume.
Wear this red skirt stamped with golden designs,
while I draw henna on Your feet.
Don this lovely purple shawl,
a charming golden necklace,
and a strand of enormous pearls.

Beloved, after I adorn You
　　with a garland of forest flowers,
　　　　behold Yourself in the mirror.
To see You chills my heart and eyes.
Now eat some dried fruits and sweets –
　　let me feed You with my own hands.
Sings Vishnu Das,
"This is the fruit of grace:
　　To everyday praise Your Child Lila."

After-ornamentation Praise:
Raga Vilaval

With loving understanding,
I now explain the essence of the nectar path
　　of beautiful Krishna's seva.
His garments are outstanding.
His crooked turban is well tied
　　and adorned with a peacock feather.
Krishna wears a strand of large pearls
　　and a gunja bead necklace.
A pendant hangs by His heart.
　　He wears red pants and has henna on His feet.
After the adornment is completed,
　　Krishna looks at Himself repeatedly in the mirror
　　　　while Harirayaji smiles.

Gwal and Palna

During the period of Gwal (only performed in the homes of Shri Vallabhacharya's lineage holders), Shri Krishna is honored as a cowlad. Before going out to graze His cows with the other cowlads, He is offered the creamy froth of fresh milk. In Shri Navanita Priyaji's temple, Child Krishna is swung in a cradle (*palna*) after ornamentation is completed.

Raga Ramkali

Mother Yashoda, this is my daily routine:
daily adorning Your son.
I wake in the morning and, while swinging him in the cradle,
sing about how He tipped over Your dairy cart.
The Gopis now make Him dance
to the beat of their clapping hands.
Sings Askarana, "Krishna is my clever Enchanter.
Beholding His face, I experience perfect contentment."

Child Lila:
Raga Asavari

My dear Hari speaks so very sweetly.
Wandering in the courtyard, His anklets chime.
Krishna's tilak is made with khol.
He wears a short necklace.
His shawl is bright yellow.
Sings Paramananda Das,
"I follow the Krishna whom the Gopis
swing in a cradle."

Rajbhog

At about midday, mother Yashoda calls Krishna home for the main meal of the day, called Rajbhog. Rajbhog can also be a picnic brought out to Krishna in the forest by His beloved Gopis. Sometimes Krishna goes to a Gopi's home for Rajbhog. The Rajbhog lunch offering is a wondrous array of sumptuous foods, including dairy products, sweets, vegetables, grains and beans. After the meal is served and Krishna has been given time to thoroughly accept and enjoy the offerings, the darshan opens, and poems are sung in praise of Shri Krishna's amazing midday lilas. Chita Swami exquisitely described Shri Krishna's forest picnic with His cowlad friends:

Shri Krishna, son of Nanda,
*   is sitting in the shade of tree enjoying His lunch.*
He is accompanied by His cowlads friends,
*   who are all looking after Him.*
Kanhaiya, the dark lovely Lord,
*   mixes some curds and rice on a leafplate,*
*   then smiles and asks for more.*
He relishes the various preparations –
*   all beyond comparison, indescribable –*
*   joyfully sent by mother Yashoda.*
Sings Chita Swami, "This Mountain Holder Krishna
*   shines in the circle of friends.*
He enchants everyone.
*   Gazing at Him, I celebrate and offer it all."*

Rajbhog Bower Lila:
Raga Sarang

Hari sits with Radha in a forest hut,
*   filled with His own delight.*
Picking up His flute, He presses it to His lips
*   and plays the Sarang raga.*
Krishna – extremely enchanting, exceptionally clever, a treasure
of virtues –
*   intentionally plays an incorrect note!*
Beloved Radha – an ocean of arts and exceedingly talented,
*   catches His mistake.*
Taking Her vina, with Her entirely fresh and lovely being
*   She plays the melody correctly.*

Impressed, Mountain Holder Krishna removes His garland and
  presents it to His Beloved, showering Her with praise,
  "Bravo! Bravo! You are elegant and so very pleasing."

Rajbhog Hot Season:
Raga Sarang

Beloved, it is good You have come at high noon.
The day, the moment, the hour, the time,
  the stars – everything is so auspicious.
A mass of bliss has arisen and
  removes the anguish of my separation.
I have made some sandalwood paste
  to anoint You with. I fall at Your feet.
Sings Tansen, "Be kind to me!
  Turn this withered limb into
    a blooming green vine."

Rajbhog Arati:
Raga Sarang

The Gopis are soaked with pleasure
  as they watch the arati lights being waved around
    Krishna, Delighter of the Gopis.
Lovely Lalita and other Gopis hold the arati plate,
  embedded with jewels, and ignite camphor lights.
The dalliance with Radha within the forest bower
  creates a mass of bliss.
Many delicacies are enjoyed there,
  and Their tastes are renewed.
"Supreme Bliss has arisen,"
  sings the ever-new Vitthaldas.
    "Gopal has conferred a bit of His bliss."

Utthapan

After a nap in the forest, Shri Krishna arises and prepares for His afternoon lilas.

Raga Nat

Krishna's friends, Subala and Shri Dama
*   call out to their cowlad friends,*
"Arjuna! Sound the conch!
*   Awake Shri Krishna – it is time to head home."*
More cowlads play and sing sweetly close by,
*   while deep in the forest bower, the Son of Nanda awakes*
*   and enjoys some betel nut and fruit.*
The Govardhan Hill, Hari's follower,
*   fulfills every desire and relieves the anguish of Shri Gokul.*
Sings the poet Paramananda Das,
"Krishna moves towards Gokul, twirling a lotus by its stem,
*   increasing ultimate joy."*

Bhog

Shri Krishna is offered fruits by the 'Pulindi' tribal women devotees. Then He prepares to herd His cows home, ending the day-long separation of His bhaktas who anxiously await His return.

Raga Nat

The Beloved is found only through love.
Physical beauty, good virtues, fine character
*   and a noble home --*
*   these will never please the Lord.*

You could have a high birth,
> *good karmas, auspicious signs,*
>> *and knowledge of the Vedas and Puranas.*
Sings Govinda, "But, my friend! Without love,
> *what is the point of reciting like a parrot?"*

Sandhya Arati

Shri Krishna returns home with His cows in the late afternoon. The Blessed Lord is offered foods, and the Arati lights are waved around Him as He delights His bhaktas with His blissful presence.

Raga Gori

His stride pleases the Gopis.
> *It is late afternoon.*
Krishna is embellished by the circle of cowlad friends.
His body is covered with the dust
> *raised by His cows.*
He wears a peacock crown,
> *a necklace of gunja beads, and a yellow shawl.*
His flute sounds a melodious song.
Sings Chaturbhujadas,
"When Giridhari arrives home from the forest,
> *Mother Yashoda greets Him*
>> *and waves the arati lights."*

Raga Gori

O, friend! Krishna is crooked!
Even His hair is crooked.
> *He strolls with lazy feet.*
His gait while strolling with the Gopis is crooked.

His brow is crooked – it is curved, and moves.
He plays a crooked tune on His flute.
With a crooked cane in hand,
      He herds His cows and calls out to them, "Hataka!"
Sings Nandadas,
"When the Gopis see their crooked Lord,
      they celebrate and flirt with Him."

Shayan

Shri Krishna is offered dinner, and after the evening Arati lights are waved, He is put to rest. Actually, Shri Krishna never really sleeps, but resides forever playing in the Lila abode. His pitcher is filled with fresh water and His snack box is always filled with sweets or dried fruits. Every moment of seva is filled with concern for Him. Krishna relates perfectly to the Gopis as a Lover and to His mother as a Child. The following poem is sung just after Shri Krishna has enjoyed the evening offerings.

Raga Kalyan

O, Radha! Take this lovely betel-leaf
      which Mohan has sent you from His own mouth.
Listen to the message from the Lord of your life.
      Why hesitate? Come closer!
Open your veil, and fill your eyes with His vision.
      Now let's go, follower of the Beloved.
Kumbhandas implores,
      "When you embrace the Mountain Holder,
            your heart will be cooled."

Evening Praise:
Raga Nayaki

My heart is stuck to that Cowherder,
the beautiful Shyam.
My days and nights don't pass.
How can I restrain this yearning heart?
He stops me along the narrow path
and harasses me with His gang of cowlad friends.
Sings Krishna Jivan, "I have been swindled by that Lord of Lakshmi.
I am no longer aware of my body."

After the evening arati lights are waved, poems concerning Radha and Krishna's intimate bedtime lilas are sung. In the following poem, Govindadas describes a moment of Shri Radha's annoyance in love with Shri Krishna.

Raga Vihag

(A Gopi tries to convince Shri Radha):
O, Radha! Shri Krishna is waiting for you
in the bower palace.
Speak to Him – your Lord of enjoyment.
Beloved of life, go to Him.
He is so anxious. Now get up and embrace Him!
O, Beloved! I will rejoice when you leave
this bittersweet annoyance,
Forget this anger and adorn yourself!
Take this mirror and behold your face –
Your beauty banishes a billion cupids.
Now, wear this blue sari.
Sings Govinda, "In the love play, an ocean of nectar arises.
Put your arms around His neck and embrace Him!
Bring that Mountain Holder under your control.

After Radha's annoyance has been broken there come songs of union.

Today Shri Radha is wandering, full of joy.
Her Govinda, the dark Moon, is filled with nectar.
Nearby, a cuckoo sings a lovely song.
Shri Radha dons a blue sari and golden necklace.
Mirror in hand, she weighs her beauty.
Sings Shri Bhatt, "Taking Krishna's own position,
she breaks the constraints of proper conduct."

Raga Vihag

Young Krishna is with the fresh Radha,
Her body fair and lovely.
Their bed is immaculate –
fragrant, cool and embedded with jewels.
Her body bears the mark of His teeth.
Radha has a betel-leaf in her mouth
and is filled with the flavor of His loving nectar.
Sings Chaturbhujadas,
"Everywhere waves arise in the ocean of love.
The delightful Radha and the enjoyer Giridhar
have defeated the love-god!

After the evening seva is complete and Shri Krishna has been put to Lila rest, bhaktas sing songs about devotional refuge and humility.

Chakai bird![4]
Fly now to the reservoir of the Lord's feet,
where there is no separation from love –
where the oblivion of darkness never prevails.
It is a sea of joyous union.

---

[4] The chakai is the female ruddy goose, a female ostrich.

There, Sanaka[5] resides as a swan,
*   celestial singers are the fish,*
*   and Krishna's toenails shine as the sun.*
There, blooming lotuses never fear the moon,[6]
*   and black bees hum the sweet Vedas.*
In that lake, blessed liberated pearls
*   imbibe the pure waters of glory.*
Oh silly bird!
Why would you ever leave that lake?
*   What are you doing here?*
In that lake, thousands of Lakshmis
*   are always making splendid lila.*
Sings Surajadas,
"Now, I have no taste for anything petty.
*   My hopes lie in that lake."*

Raga Vihag

Live by the Govardhan Hill, and place your mind
*   at the feet of enchanting Gopal.*
When I roll in the sands of Vraj,
*   my body bristles with joy.*
Then I bathe in Govinda Lake.
Sings Rasika Pritam, "I tell Shri Krishna
*   what is good for the heart."*

---

[5] Sanaka and his three brothers are celibate sages who continually wander around for the benefit of humanity, always appearing as five year olds.

[6] The lotus fears the moon, because when the moon appears at night, the lotus closes.

A Song of Refuge
Raga Vihag

Shri Vallabh, I take your shelter.
Just by seeing you, my sorrow is suspended.
      My pleasure has become boundless.
You received the command from Shri Krishna
      to reunite souls with Brahma Sambandha mantra.
You reveal Krishna Lila and teach
      the joyful practice of seva.
Shri Vallabh, you churned the nectar of the Shrimad Bhagavata
      and have shown the grace filled way.
Such is the nature of the mighty Vallabh.
      You fulfill my heart.

8.

UTSAVAS:
SHRI KRISHNA'S FESTIVE YEAR

"We experience Krishna with our eyes. We feel Him through all of our senses. Hari is the desire – the festival of our hearts. To imbibe Krishna's form is the ultimate reward."

— Venu Gita, Subodhini

In the Path of Grace, bhaktas daily celebrate Shri Krishna's form and Lila, but festive days provide a special opportunity to rejoice over Him. Some festivals recreate the lilas Lord Krishna performed here on earth, such as the swing festival of *Hindola*, and the celebration of *Annakut*, when Shri Krishna is offered a mountain of food and an exceptional variety of foods. Other festivals like *Makar Sankranti* are of Vedic origin, while some festivals have their roots in local traditions. The entire forty day season of Basant is considered to be a festival. Every three years an extra month called *Adhik Maas* is added to the calendar, during which time any festival of the year can be celebrated on any day!

Bhaktas are always looking forward to celebrating Krishna. The Sanskrit word *utsava* not only means festival, but also carries the meaning of delight, merriment and pleasure. Utsavas elevate the mood of the bhakta and of Shri Krishna as well! Krishna is always in a festive mood. The Ashta Chhap singer Chaturbhujadas sings,

My friend! Today, tomorrow, and every day,
He is new and different, always more and more.

Behold nectar-filled Krishna, the Mountain Holder!
His splendor is new every moment.
What poet can possibly describe His clothes and ornaments?

The Indian calendar distinguishes six seasons: spring, summer, monsoon, autumn, early winter and winter. Each is duly glorified in Shri Krishna's seva. The ragas, ornaments and food offerings all vary according to these seasons, the time of day and Lila. The variations of season provide an additional source of inspiration, an atmosphere to accommodate the Lord's various lilas. Seva carries a great sensitivity to nature and its relationship with the Divine. In summer Shri Krishna enjoys fountains and water plays. In winter He is warmed with a coal stove and snuggled in silk quilts. Every season brings its own inherent joy and the opportunity to nourish the firm mood of devotion.

Whatever the season – spring, summer, monsoon, autumn, early winter or winter, Krishna's homes are filled with joy and merriment. Hardly a week passes without a celebration. Festivals often herald the changing of the seasons, and special celebrations are held on the birthdays of Shri Vallabhacharya, Shri Gusainji as well as their descendants. Days which mark significant events in the history of the lineage are also honored.

The six different seasons represent the Blessed Lord's six attributes. Summer is Shri Krishna's quality of lordship. The rainy season holds His valor, autumn His fame and the beginning of winter, His wealth. The second phase of winter, called *shishira*, is knowledge. The king of all seasons, spring, is His virtue of renunciation. Shri Krishna is *Dharmi*, the One who holds all divine virtues.

Regardless of origin, every festival is transformed and acquires divine significance when it falls within the orbit of Shri Krishna's blessed worship. As seva is an act of love, every celebration enriches that bhakti mood and begs the chance for the Blessed One to shower His boundless grace. A celebration is something to look forward to; then it is enjoyed, and lastly, remembered. In Shri Nathji's temple, the celebration of Krishna's appearance, *Janmashtami*, begins a one month before the actual day! The pre-celebration increases divine anticipation, heightens and prolongs the celebration. The celebratory mood maintains the flow of nectar and gives bhaktas the chance to participate and savor the Krishna experience. When it elicits a divine response, then it is known that Shri Krishna has joined the celebrations.

On festive days, Shri Krishna is adorned with special garments and praised with related songs. The utsava seva was greatly enhanced by Shri Gusainji, who added his own unique Vrindavan flavor to the festive mood. He took whatever was supreme in the Vedic tradition, in the world, and in Krishna's divine realms, incorporating it all into an elaborate and sensitive system of worship. He introduced inspiring elements that he found in the royal homes of India. The paintings, food offerings, garments and other items used in the seva all became part of the ultimate sacrifice. Everything is used to please Shri Krishna, who appears before His bhaktas according to the way they worship Him.

Each season brings different types of cloth, paintings, poetry, melodies, poems, perfumes and food offerings. There are fifty-two major festivals during the year, but the bhakta's mood makes this festive number infinite. The gurus of the Path of Grace are the Gopis; they are the enlightened festival performers. Blessed bhaktas emulate their bhavas, for they are not only the perfect devotional models – they are also the inner festival of Shri Krishna's heart.

Each quarter of the year is associated with one of Krishna's most beloved Gopis: Radha (also known as Shri Swaminiji), Shri Chandravali, Shri Lalita and Shri Yamunaji.

We will begin the utsava section with Shri Radha's quarter, covering the months of Shravan, Bhadrapada and Ashvin, (corresponding roughly to August, September and October.) This quarter, which begins with the monsoon season, is very romantic and beloved to Shri Krishna, so it is only natural that it belongs to His most cherished Shri Radha. Many *pichvais* (paintings on cloth which hang behind Shri Krishna in His temple) are offered in the seva during this season. They depict peacocks, the pouring rains and green groves of Vrindavan. These images all support and nourish the mood of love's union. Green, in all its varying shades, dominates the color scheme.

The poetry sung in this season describes the beauty of the season and reinforces the romantic mood. The exquisite monsoon Malhar raga is featured in this season. As Surdas tells us, "The pleasures of singing of Gopal are not equaled by mantra recitations, austerities or by bathing in millions of holy places." Poems in the Path of Grace describe Krishna's festivals and reveal the way the Gopis celebrated over Him. They can also contain practical bhakti advice. The grace filled compositions sung before Shri Krishna are all composed by realized beings – the Ashta Chhap poets and other bhaktas who have come face to face with the Lord of Sweetness. They reveal the bhakta's inner reality and are encoded in a Lila language that can only be fully understood by one who has entrance into the Path. A careful review of the words of the poets provides glimpses of Shri Krishna's festive playground.

The Path of Grace emulates the selfless love of the Gopis and follows their footsteps through the lovely groves of Vrindavan. The sublime celebratory method they demonstrated is to connect to the divine source while living in this world, and then to live off His *prasad* – His causeless grace. Then the heart becomes addicted to nectar. Shri

Krishna's celebrations all enhance this devotional mood.

The dates of the festivals are fixed by the Vedic lunar calendar, with the exception of Makar Sankranti, which is based on the solar calendar and falls on January 14th of every year. Each lunar month has a dark half (from full to new moon) and bright half (from new to full moon). In Vedic terminology, the dark half, *Krishna paksh* begins at purnima and leads to amavas. *Shukla paksh* begins at amavas and culminates in purnima. Now follows a short review of some of the main celebrations in the Path of Grace:

THE SWING SEASON
Shravan Krishna 1 – Bhadrapad Krishna 3

During this month of union (roughly August), Shri Krishna plays with all of His bhaktas in Vrindavan by the door of His Lila bower, filling His bhaktas with His inner nectar. Every day for one month following Shravan Krishna 1, Shri Krishna sits in a *Hindola* – a swing. Hindolas can be painted, studded with jewels or mirrors, decorated with fruits or flowers, or can be made of silver or even gold. Shri Harirayaji explains,

Raga Vihaga

Swing, swing, swing –
*   Beloved Krishna, swing!*
A golden Hindola stands by Yamuna's banks,
*   surrounded by lovely blossoming trees and vines.*
Rasika Pritam sings, "When I see this,
*   the pains of my heart are relieved."*

Raga Vihaga

They swing together, arm in arm.
Look by the door of the fresh forest bower –
      see the splendor all around!
Krishna first plays a full scale on His flute,
      then plays a protracted tone,
           and then softens the note.
Sings Swami Haridas,
"Radha plays in Krishna's bower.
      When I behold that divine beauty,
         I give everything else away."

HARIYALI AMAVAS
Shravan Krishna 15

This monsoon season festival is noteworthy for its imaginative use of the color green. On this day, all the Lord's garments are green. The coverings of Shri Krishna's seat and cushions are all green. His ornaments are studded with emeralds and precious green stones. The Hindola is adorned with green leaves. Pistachio and other green foods are offered on this day, and the songs that are sung in front of Shri Krishna praise the green monsoon season. A song by Shri Harirayaji Mahaprabhu is sung on this day and conveys the mood of this festival,

O, friend! Shravan, the green season is here.
      The earth is green –
the flowering trees and bowers, His garments –
      even Hari's crown is green!

THAKURANI TEEJ
Shravan Shukla 3

This festival has its origins in the royal homes of Rajasthan, but in Shri Krishna's temples, the day is dedicated to Shri Radha. Shri Krishna swings in a wooden Hindola embedded with mirrors. The painted pichvai shows dark monsoon clouds, rain and streaks of lightning. The poet Surdas describes the lila:

Raga Malhar

How can I come?
> *These rain drops will soak my sari.*
First the clouds thunder,
>> *then the wind howls,*
>>> *and thirdly, it is as dark as night.*
O, Krishna! I am fair and delicate.
>> *Secondly, I have a pot of curds on my head.*
>>> *Thirdly, the Yamuna River is flooded.*
Sings Surdas, "When Radha's nose ring gets caught in her sari,
> *young Krishna comes to her aid."*

PAVITRA EKADASHI
Shravan Shukla 11

This is the day on which Shri Krishna appeared before Shri Vallabhacharya at Thakurani Ghat in Shrimad Gokul and instructed him to initiate divine souls with the Brahma Sambandha mantra. After the soul's connection with Shri Krishna, all impurities are removed, and the soul becomes bound to Krishna. On this day, Shri Krishna is adorned with a *pavitra*, a garland of three hundred and sixty silk threads, one for each day of the year. On the following day, that pavitra is offered to one's guru.

JANMASHTAMI
Bhadrapada Krishna 8

Shri Krishna's appearance day (generally occurring in August) is one of the most important festivals of the year. On this day the Blessed Lord is bathed with milk, ghee, curds, honey and powdered sugar and adorned in saffron-colored garments, which demonstrate the great affection Shri Krishna and Shri Swaminiji share with one another. The ornaments are largely red in color, a hue that increases the excitement of the amorous mood. Shri Krishna's necklaces are really the forms of His bhaktas, and that is why He wears them near His heart.

Shri Krishna wears peacock feathers and a tiger's claw locket, which wards off the evil eye. Lotus motifs are drawn on Shri Krishna's cheeks with a saffron paste. Krishna's appearance takes place at midnight. All the Gopis come and make secret offerings to their Beloved. Krishna's entrance into the world of matter is strictly to shower grace over His bhaktas.

Raga Kanharo

The moment Shri Krishna was born, there was joy.
Krishna is full of the nine jewels of life
         and removes every suffering.
Vasudeva and Devaki construct a cradle
         and swing infant Krishna.
Then, with a lion's roar,
         Vasudeva crosses the Yamuna River
           and walks towards Gokul.
There, Nanda and Yashoda's hearts are ecstatic
         when they find their newborn Krishna.
           They summon the sage, Garga.

Paramananda Das proclaims,
"Krishna has been born in Gokul!"

NANDAMAHOTSAVA
Bhadrapada Krishna 9

Nanda Mahotsava is celebrated on the day following Shri Krishna's appearance day. This ecstatic festival recreates the celebrations which took place in the home of Nanda and Yashoda in Gokul. Joy overflows as everyone's desires are fulfilled by the presence of Shri Krishna in their lives. Child Krishna is swung in a cradle, and even today, the male lineage holders dress up as Yashoda and swing their Beloved Krishna, while the *Mukhiyaji* (head assistant in the worship) dons a fake beard and becomes Nanda Baba. Milk and curd mixed with turmeric are splashed over everyone as they sing and dance in the festive celebration.

Raga Sarang

Today, Krishna's father Nanda is delighted.
The Gopis dance, make merry
        and sing auspicious songs.
They wear red and yellow blouses and
        new saris lined with pearls.
They have anointed themselves
        with chova and sandalwood paste
                and have drawn red powder
                        in the parts of their hair.
The cowlads bring butter, milk and curds in large pots,
        while flutes and horns sound in tune with lovely songs.
Turmeric, grass, rice, curd and kumkum powder
        are thrown everywhere, muddying the courtyard.
Everyone laughs and embraces each other,
        their hearts overjoyed with love.

Great sages recite the four Vedas
    while the five sounds join the drum.
"In Gokul," sings Paramananda Das,
    "Supreme Bliss increases.
            The joyous, happy heart is delighted."

RADHASHTAMI
Bhadrapada Shukla 8

Shri Krishna's most beloved, Shri Radha, appears on this day (often in September). She is two years older than Shri Krishna, and it is said that she refused to open her eyes until He was born. Her very first vision was the sight of Shri Krishna! The jewelry and cloth Krishna wears on this day are similar to that of His own appearance day, for Shri Radha is His inner form. Her manifestation is full of nectar. Many special preparations and songs are offered on sacred festive day. Shri Gusainji calls the name of Radha "the secret inner essence of the Vedas."

DAAN
Bhadrapada Shukla 11 to the new moon

Shri Krishna does nothing unless it is connected to nectar, and so in the Daan Lila, He stops the Swaminis and demands a tax on their dairy products (their secret forms of nectar).

Raga Kalyan

O, Krishna, since when have You began
    this tax on our curds?
You broke my pot and snapped my necklace,
    but I know Your heart.
Listen Queen Yashoda, I follow Nanda's rule.
Askaran's Lord is the clever Mohan,
    an ocean of virtue – and very proud.

Bhadrapad Shukla 12 is the appearance day of Lord Vaman, Vishnu's dwarf incarnation who asked for three steps of land from Bali Raja. Lord Vaman then fooled Bali Raja by taking on a cosmic form, covering all the worlds in two strides and placing His third step on Bali Raja's head. In this way Hari accepted Bali Raja's offerings. Lord Vaman is the avatar of action.

SANJHI
From Bhadrapada Shukla 15

From Bhadrapada Shukla 15 onwards, (generally in September) Shri Krishna and His bhaktas celebrate Sanjhi Lila for fifteen days. Sanjhi are large flower arrangements decorating the floor, often covering half of the temple courtyard. They are placed before Shri Krishna during the afternoon darshans. Sometimes Sanjhi Lila and Daan Lila are combined, and Gopis with pots on their heads become part of the Sanjhi Lila. Sanjhis can also be made of dried fruits, leaves, or powdered colors that can even be sprinkled on the surface of water in trays. On the Lila level, during Sanjhi Shri Krishna sometimes dresses up as a Gopi and goes out to pick flowers with the other Gopis, in hopes of some special meeting with His dear ones.

Raga Gori

I came alone at sunset to gather flowers.
>*Krishna, as You head home with the cows,*
>>*I am lucky to meet You.*
In front of me is a mass of dark rain clouds.
>*I can no longer see the path.*
My Chundari sari will bleed from the rain drops.
>*O, Krishna! Protect me from these showers.*

The lightning bolts are blindingly bright.
　　I am so afraid, and You are so unattached.
　　　Take me with You – embrace me.
Surdas sings, "O, Enchanter! People say You are virtuous.
　　Now don't be so prideful –
　　　　place Your black blanket over me."

MAHA RASA
Ashvin Shukla 15

On this autumnal full moon night Shri Krishna dances Rasa with the Gopis; it is one of the main festivals of the year. In the Rasa dance, the Gopis discover a congregation of nectars and unite their souls, mind-hearts, speech, prana, senses and bodies with Shri Krishna. They have waited a long time for this experience. Now they are blessed and are able to dance with their Beloved in this world; it is the supreme reward.

Shri Krishna is dressed in a silver brocaded dance skirt called *kaachhani*. All His ornaments are of diamonds. The pichvai painting that hangs behind Shri Krishna depicts the Rasa Lila. On this day all the utensils to be used are silver. Even the foods and the beverages served are white. The main offering is rice pudding, which is placed out in the full moonlight. Everything used in the seva blends into the silver beams of the full moonlight. The sight of Shri Krishna's dance is reserved for His chosen few.

Raga Iman

By the banks of the Yamuna
　　on the autumn night,
Krishna and the desirous Radha dance
　　to the beat of the drum:
Tri tata tri tata gira gira gira
　　Dhi dhi talang jhan jhan jhan janana janana.

The upanga plays, and Krishna enjoys the sounds.
    Ta tirka ta ta tatatat tatatat.
Radhe sings and is more lovely
    than a million loves.
Krishnadas describes the glory of that dance,
    while Radha and Krishna dance
to the sound of the mridangam drum:
    Karta te karta te, kankrite kankrite.

Shri Lalita Gopi takes care of the next three months of seva: *Kartik, Margashirsh* and *Poush* (the approximate equivalents of November, December and January). These are the first days of winter. Shri Krishna is adorned in heavily brocaded clothes and ornaments. Even the pichvais are extensively brocaded and embroidered with gold and silver thread. Strong and rich colors are preferred.

DIWALI
Kartik Krishna 15

This major festival of the quarter marks the end of the Hindu calendar year. Shri Krishna wears clothes of silver brocade and a fan-shaped plume of peacock feathers. His ornaments are made from diamonds, rubies and emeralds. Cows are also ornamented and brought into the temple. For some days before this festival, Shri Krishna sits in a *Hatari*, a pavilion of mirrors where Krishna sells various sweets and other goods and tries to attract the Gopis. He bargains in the currency of love. The bhakta poet Paramananda Das sings of the occasion:

Raga Kanharo

Today is the auspicious day of Diwali.
The Vraj ladies gather and sing auspicious songs.
They decorate the courtyard by the auspicious gate.
Fruits, nuts, sweets and fried foods
*   are brought on a golden tray.*
Paramananda Das follows Shri Krishna,
*   who is adorned with precious garments and jewels.*

ANNAKUTA
Kartik Shukla 1

This festival takes place on the day after Diwali and is the most renowned festival of the Pushti Marg. It is the day when Shri Krishna persuaded the inhabitants of Vraj to worship the Govardhan Hill and cows instead of Indra, the rain god. Then Shri Krishna Himself became the Govardhan Hill, and with a thousand arms, enjoyed all the offerings. In a jealous wrath, Indra showered destructive rains on Vraj, and Shri Krishna lifted the entire Govardhan Hill with one finger, protecting everyone. In this Lila, Shri Krishna directs the bhaktas' worship away from the material divinities, towards the Supreme Brahman.

To this day, a huge mountain of rice and many other items are all offered to Shri Krishna. Cows are beautifully decorated with peacock feathers on their heads and brought into the temple, with anklet bells tied to their hooves. The backs of the cowherds and the cows are marked with red handprints, for red is the color of love.

Raga Sarang

See Hari eat with a thousand arms.
Over there He is talking with the Gopis.
Lalita says to Radha, "See, there He is!
The One who inhabits your heart."
Blessed are all those who live
with the Lord of Gokul.
Nanda is elated to see Him eat.
All the men and women of Gokul are also full of joy.
Sings Surdas, "Krishna is an ocean of bliss and full of virtue.
Now He dances to the beat of the Gopis' clapping hands."

PRABODHINI EKADASHI
Kartik Shukla 11

The day after Diwali, the gods are awakened from four
months of deep slumber. The marriage of a *shaligrama* – a
round black stone form of Vishnu – to Tulsi, the sacred basil
plant, is celebrated in a *mandap* constructed with stalks of
sugarcane. The shaligrama is bathed with ghee, honey, sugar,
milk and curd. Poems of marriage are sung throughout the
night.

"O, Mother! I want a wife like that charming Radha
who comes to our home wearing jingling anklets.
She will cook delicious food for me and serve me well.
She will fan me and veil herself before father Nanda Baba.
Then she will hold me in her lap and captivate me."
Yashoda replies, "Beloved son – now go and tell your father.
He will arrange for that marriage."
Sings Chaturbhuja, "When Yashoda and Nanda Baba hear
Child Krishna's words, a congregation of pleasure arises.
Their hearts are overwhelmed with joy."

SHRI GUSAINJI'S BIRTHDAY
Poush Krishna 9

Shri Gusainji, also known as Shri Vitthalnathji, is Shri Krishna's incarnation and the son of Shri Vallabhacharya. He embellished Shri Krishna's seva in the Path of Grace and composed a great volume of Sanskrit literature. His devotional contributions are immense, and his appearance day, (usually in December) is among the most celebrated Pushti Marg festivals of the year.

Raga Sarang

Shri Vitthalnathji's lotus feet purify the three worlds.
I look, touch and bow to them again and again.
Supremely beautiful Shri Vitthalnathji
contains the power of the Mountain Holder.
He appears as a human for the benefit of the saints
and to reveal the inner Lila.
He is the moon of Vrindavan.
A ghost who took a drop of water that touched his feet
was immediately liberated.
You are a Lord full of compassion,
a treasure of bliss.
Bhagavandas explains, "Your play is continuous.
Lord of enjoyers, Victory! Victory!
The Shrutis sing your glories."

Shri Chandravali presides over the months of *Magh*, *Phalgun* and *Chaitra* (approximately February, March and April). These are the spring months, traditionally associated with Kamadeva, the love-god.

VASANT PANCHAMI AND THE FORTY DAYS OF HOLI
Magh Shukla 5 – Chaitra Krishna 1

Holi celebrates the arrival of spring. It begins with Vasant Panchami, the birthday of Kamadeva. For forty days afterwards, red and white powders, a dark fragrant liquid made of sandalwood resin, called chova, and sandalwood paste are sprinkled over and around Shri Krishna. During Holi, Shri Krishna plays in unrestricted ways with all of His bhaktas. This is considered to be Shri Krishna's favorite festival. He wears mostly white during these days so that the colors His bhaktas throw at Him will show. Krishna loves this festival so much that the day after it is over, great efforts are taken to make Him forget it!

Raga Basant

Tell me the truth, Enchanter of my heart!
*   Only then will I play Holi with you.*
O, Mohan! Where were you last night?
*   What misdeeds did you commit?*
Your face has red stains of her betel.
The impressions of her bangles
*   are exposed on your back.*
Your chest has indentations of her necklace!
On the surface you present one image,
*   but your heart contains another,*
*   and your movements, yet another.*
Tell me clever Krishna –
*   do you think I am that foolish?*
You have shown up here in the morning
*   with some contrived story.*
Sings Surdas, "O, Lord! Don't be like that!
*   Come and meet me – why this sneaking around?*

Son of Nanda, I know you will do as you like,
*   for these are the days of Holi."*

Raga Kalyan

Shri Govardhana Lal!
With Your wide, unsteady eyes
*   and the forest garland adorning Your chest,*
*   You enchant all the women of Vraj.*
Frolicking playfully, Krishna reaches the path the Gopis walk
*   on their way to fetch water.*
He tips the jugs off the Gopis' heads
*   and won't let them draw water from the well.*
Krishna, the darling Son of Nanda, plays in this way.
The Vraj Gopis' hearts are filled with joy
*   when they behold His face.*
Beloved Krishna has covered His hands
*   with red vermillion powder.*
He stealthily sneaks up behind the Gopis,
*   smears their cheeks, and dashes away.*
In this way, Krishna plays the spring sport of Holi with the Gopis.
*   Govinda's people rejoice over Shri Nathji's form.*

Raga Vihaga

Krishna is an Enjoyer and loves the month of spring.
The Vraj Bhaktas tie white and red powder into their cloths.
*   They run and grab hold of each other's faces.*
They sing insults and show their love.
*   The Holi colors become a descending rain.*
Sings Krishna Jivan, "They make Krishna dance in so many ways."

DOLOTSAVA
Chaitra Krishna 1

This festival takes place on the day after Holi, (usually some time in March) when the demoness Holika is burnt. Shri Krishna and His Beloved sit in a Dol swing that is decorated with mango blossoms and other flowers. This is a Kunja Lila, taking place in the divine inner bower. On this day there are four separate swing darshans, and the throwing of color reaches its zenith. Krishna is dressed in all white. Dol is the grand finale of the spring Vasant festival.

Raga Kalyan

The Gopis swing Krishna in the Dol swing.
Lalita and other Gopis behold Radha's Husband
          and put chova, sandalwood paste, and red powder on Him.
The air is filled with red and white powders.
Krishna, the lotus-eyed one, eats betel pan
          and wears a garland over His heart.
The mridangam drum holds the beat; the agoti sounds.
          The flute plays so sweetly.
Nandadas hears the Gopis sing.
          Shri Gopal is delighted.

The next three months of *Vaishakh*, *Jyesth* and *Ashadh* (usually May, June and July) are the months of Shri Yamunaji's seva. Her company cools the Lord and protects Him from the scorching heat of the season. During these months, the Lord is constantly fanned and lightly dressed in fine, light cotton clothes. Flowers are abundantly used in garlands and pavilions, and fountains spray water to cool the atmosphere. White is the dominant color of this quarter.

LORD RAMA'S APPEARANCE DAY
Chaitra Shukla 9

O friend, Lord Rama has appeared!
Dasharath's sin of three murders
was absolved when he heard
the charming name of Rama.
During the great celebration of Rama's appearance,
the bards lose themselves.
All the residents of the earth rejoice.
The young woman break out in song.
Glories! Glories to Rama resound around the world.
The saints' hearts are delighted.
Paramananda Das celebrates the event
and takes shelter at His lotus feet.

SHRI VALLABHACHARYA'S APPEARANCE DAY
Vaishakh Krishna 11

This is perhaps the most important festival for the lineage and typically occurs in April. Songs in praise of Shri Mahaprabhu Vallabhacharya begin two weeks before this day. The very form of Shri Swaminiji, Shri Vallabhacharya manifested upon the earth to uplift divine souls. He taught his disciples to love Shri Krishna in the devotional mood of the Gopis of Vrindavan. Shri Acharyaji coupled a pure non-dualist philosophy with divine appreciation and gifted his intimate ones the experience of Shri Krishna's Lila.

Raga Sarang

Shri Vallabhacharya is wearing
a saffron-colored dhoti and shawl.

Tilaks and mudras adorn his body.
He sits at his father, Lakshman's home; it is his birthday.
From head to toe, his form conveys amazing experience.
His beauty vanquishes a million loves.
      He is the zenith of loveliness.
The power of his brilliance is without limit.
      Nearby, divine women sing Lila praises.
Padmanabhdas sees Shri Krishna as Vallabh, the Lord of speech.
      Those who were there are truly fortunate.

Raga Kanharo

The Lila would become old if Shri Vallabh did not appear;
      the earth would become barren.
Everyday, Shri Vallabh's beauty is new,
      like an exceptional jewel set in gold.
Sagunadas sings, "I am a follower of his home.
      His glories are sung by the sages."

YAMUNA DASHAMI
Jyesht Krishna 10

This festival, (occurring in May) honors the divine River and Goddess Shri Yamunaji. Shri Nathji is dressed in a white *adbandh* – a light cloth reaching from His waist to His knees, a white turban and pearls. A song from the Gita Govinda is sung which describes Krishna's water sports in the River Yamuna:

In the woods on the windswept Yamuna banks,
      Krishna waits....
He calls your name on His sweet reed flute.
      He cherishes breeze-blown pollen
            that has touched your delicate body.

SNAN YATRA
Jyesth Shukla 15

On this day in the middle of the hot season (usually falling in May), Shri Krishna wears a light dhoti, an uparna on His shoulders, and pearled ornaments. The public are allowed the unique opportunity to behold Him being bathed with cool water poured through a conch. Shri Krishna is offered 125,000 mangoes, an auspicious number of the season's most luscious fruit.

9.
SHRI KRISHNA'S SACRED FORMS

"Always reflect on Hari's form with conviction. See and touch Him clearly. Make every movement always for Him." (*Nirodha Lakshana*: Bound by Hari, 17)

In the Path of Grace, Shri Krishna appears in innumerable ways to fulfill the desires of His bhaktas, according to each one's devotional sentiments. He is the Lord of Sweetness and makes everything sweet. Shri Krishna's form, Lila and inner mood are only accessible when the mind and heart become bound to Him. The worship of Shri Krishna's svarupa (the adoration of His divine form), allows the sensitive bhakta a rare chance to experience Him within this world. Blessed bhaktas are *nirguna* – that is, they live beyond the effects of the material creation and are full of His divine presence.

If Brahman remained abstract, there would be no way to garland Him with flowers. If He had no feet, how could He run with the cows? If He had no face, then there would be nothing to look forward to. In the Path of Grace, the transcendent Lord becomes a Child or a Lover and then plays with His bhaktas.

The supreme reward is to experience Shri Krishna here, with one's God-given senses. Shri Krishna is a householder and enjoys living within a devotional family who dedicate everything to Him. Bhaktas live on His prasad – His free-flowing grace in the form of foods and anything else which He has been offered and enjoyed. The Supreme may be infinite, without beginning or end, but He takes on a delightful form for the sake of His bhaktas. In their company, Shri Krishna becomes complete.

All of the Shri Krishna svarupas in the Path of Grace are equally Krishna. The main svarupas of Shri Gusainji's household are still worshipped with deep devotion and attentive care by his descendants. These Krishna svarupas vary in size, color, form and Lila, but they all share a common connection to Shri Vallabhacharya and his son, Shri Gusainji. Each is self-manifested, having appeared directly from fire, water or the earth. They have provided numerous souls with direct divine experiences, and to have their darshan is indeed auspicious.

Shri Gusainji arranged for separate households for his seven sons and provided each with his own Krishna svarupa. His eldest son, Shri Girdharji, received the seva of Shri Mathuradheesh. Shri Girdharji thus became the Adi-Grihadheeshwar or original Tilkayat of the First House – the *Pratham Peeth*. Shri Girdharji performed Shri Mathuradheesh's seva in his own home. When Shri Gusainji left this world, Shri Girdharji inherited his father's house as well, along with the post of *Pradhan Peeth Tilkayat* – a post which is still today honored as the head of the Vallabhkul lineage – and the seva of Shri Navanita Priyaji. Shri Girdharji therefore became the head of two houses: his father, Shri Gusainji's house, as well as his own.

Shri Girdharji's eldest son, Muralidharji, returned to the eternal Lila at an early age, leaving Shri Damodarji and Shri Gopinathji to succeed him. Shri Damodarji became Pradhan Peeth Tilkayat and received the worship of Shri Navanita Priyaji. The Pradhan Peeth today is centered in Nathdvara, Rajasthan, where the seva of Shri Nathji and Shri Navanita Priyaji are maintained by the Tilkayat.

Shri Girdharji's own post as Tilkayat of the First House, and his own Nidhi savrupa, Shri Mathuradheesh

Prabhu, went to his youngest son, Shri Gopinathji. The *Pratham Peeth* is now based in Kota, Rajasthan, where Shri Mathuradheeshji resides.

Shri Gusainji's other six sons became the heads of their own seats (*Peeth*), or houses (*Grha*). To this day, these eight – the Pradhan Peeth plus the First through Seventh Houses – are each led by the descendants of Shri Gusainji and his seven sons.[7] Their ancestral homes house the main Krishna svarupas and are centers of Pushti Marg lineage, worship and culture. Each home has its own unique form of Shri Krishna, and the modes of worship vary from house to house, for Shri Krishna interacts with His bhaktas in infinite ways. Now hear about the main svarupas in Shri Vallabhacharya's Path of Grace:

SHRI NATHJI

Shri Govardhan Nathji not only affords His intimate bhaktas the experience of His inner reality, but also is the Liberator of all souls. Shri Gusainji explained Shri Nathji's divine nature to his disciple, a renounced Brahmin, thus: "Shri Nathji is the Supreme Lord of the Lila bower. He stands by the door of a cave on the Govardhan Hill and calls all of His Lila souls to Him with His raised left hand." Shri Nathji's closed right hand rests on His hip and contains His hidden nectar essence.

Shri Nathji's left hand first manifested on top of the Govardhan Hill (Girirajji) in 1410 CE. On Shri Vallabhacharya's appearance day in 1479, Shri Nathji's face emerged from Girirajji. In 1493, Shri Nathji appeared to Shri

---

[7] The term 'Peeth' came into familiar usage in the past century. The original and more accurate term for these 8 branches of Shri Gusainji's family is 'Griha,' or house.

Vallabhacharya in Jharkhand and called him to the sacred Hill to establish His seva. When Shri Vallabhacharya and his party arrived at Girirajji, Mahaprabhuji climbed the Hill and embraced Shri Nathji. He then established Shri Nathji's worship and adorned Him with a dhoti, gunja-bead necklace, and peacock feather crown. Shri Vallabhacharya named Him Gopalji, 'Keeper of the cows.' Shri Gusainji named Him Shri Govardhan Nathji, and his sons later called Him Shri Nathji, a name which continues to be used.

On Shri Nathji's left are two smaller svarupas: Madan Mohanji, a standing, flute-playing Krishna, as well as tiny Bal Krishnaji, a svarupa of infant Krishna crawling on the floor, holding a sweetball. This svarupa was found by Shri Vallabhacharya when he was bathing in the Yamuna River.

To Shri Nathji's right is a shaligrama acquired by Shri Vallabhacharya in South India and a *Girirajji Shila* – a stone from the Govardhan Hill picked up when Shri Nathji left the Govardhan Hill. There is also a single wooden sandal, called a *paduka*, which was worn by Shri Vallabhacharya. In all of the main places of worship in the Pushti Marg, other forms of Shri Krishna or items related to Shri Vallabhacharya or his descendants are established in the worship alongside the main Krishna svarupa.

SHRI NAVANITA PRIYAJI

Shri Navanita Priyaji – "the One who loves fresh butter," also affectionately called "Lalan," is a form of Child Krishna crawling on the floor with a mound of butter in His right hand. He was found in the Yamuna River near Mahavan by a Kshatriya woman and presented to Shri Vallabhacharya. Shri Navanita Priyaji was worshipped by Shri Vallabhacharya, as well as Shri Gusainji, in Gokul.

Shri Gusainji himself wished to retain the seva of Shri Navanita Priyaji as long as He remained on this earth. When he entered the eternal Lila, the seva of Shri Navanita Priyaji was inherited by his eldest son, Shri Girdharji, who later entrusted 'Lalan' to his second son, Shri Damodarji. Shri Navanita Priyaji is the Nidhi svarupa of the Pradhan Peeth.

On major festivals, Shri Navanita Priyaji sits with Shri Nathji, but He also enjoys His own separate Haveli just next to Shri Nathji's. Shri Gusainji explains, "Shri Navanita Priyaji is the form of Child Krishna who resides with Mother Yashoda. Krishna as Shri Navanita Priyaji plays like an infant in front of her."

SHRI MATHURESHJI

Shri Mathureshji, also called Shri Mathuradheesh and Mathuranathji, is a four-armed, dark form of Shri Krishna. Shri Mathureshji emerged in a gigantic form, as tall as a large tree, in the presence of Shri Vallabhacharya and his disciple, Padmanabhdas. He then became small enough to sit on the bhakti master's lap. Padmanabhdasji lovingly made Shri Mathureshji's seva, and was blessed with many divine experiences. Shri Mathuranathji was later returned to Shri Vallabhacharya. Shri Gusainji entrusted Him to his eldest son Shri Girdharji, who later presented Him to his third son, Shri Gopinathji.

Shri Mathureshji relocated to Kota, Rajasthan during Aurangzeb's reign. Today He is worshipped by descendents of Shri Girdharji, the heads of the Pratham Peeth. Shri Gusainji explained to his disciple, the renounced Brahmin, His form and Lila:

"Then, when Shri Krishna becomes a young Lad and begins to herd His cows, that form of Shri Krishna is Shri Mathuranathji. One day, Shri Mathuranath went out with

His friends to the Gopis' homes to steal butter. When He entered Shri Swaminiji's home to steal her milk, curds and butter, Shri Swamini quietly came in, grabbed the Blessed Lord with two hands, and said, 'Today, I have caught you! Now I will bring you before Nanda and Yashoda and tell them all about Your stealing.'

"At that moment, Shri Mathuranath manifested two additional arms and, with folded hands, prayed to Shri Swaminiji, 'I am under your control. Always keep Me with you. I hold this conch in My lower right hand, because it is the form of Your neck. In My upper right hand I hold a lotus, because Your face is like a lotus. In My upper left hand I hold the mace, because it is like the form of Your breast. My lower left hand holds the chakra discus; it is like the bells on Your belt. I worship the bangles on Your wrist and put them on My own wrist. Now please release Me.' When she did, He gave Her a taste of His nectar lips. This is the Lila of Shri Mathuranathji."

SHRI VITTHALNATHJI

Shri Vitthalnathji was found in the Ganges River by an ascetic, who presented Him to Shri Vallabhacharya on the day his second son, Shri Gusainji was born. Shri Vallabhacharya named both his son and the Krishna svarupa Shri Vitthalnathji. Shri Gusainji later entrusted Shri Vitthalnathji to his second son, Shri Govindaji.

Shri Vitthalnathji was brought to Kota in 1581 CE and then in 1662 to the small town of Khimnor, Rajasthan. After Shrinathji moved to Nathdvara, Shri Vitthalnathji was also brought there, and a separate Haveli was built for Him by Shri Harirayaji.

Shri Vitthalnathji is a small golden and dark svarupa with His hands resting on His hips. He is accompanied by one Swamini, who always resides to His left. Shri Gusainji explains Their divine nature thus:

"When the Gopis worshipped Shri Katyayani Devi in order to secure Shri Krishna as their Husband, Shri Krishna came to the banks of the Yamuna River, stole their clothes, and climbed up a Kadamba tree. This is the form of Shri Vitthalnathji. He remains absorbed in the bhava of Shri Swaminiji, and that is why He became Her golden color. If Shri Vitthalnathji had appeared by the banks of the Yamuna River as dark Krishna, the Gopis would have recognized Him, and He would not have been able to steal their clothes. The Gopis were delayed in meeting Krishna because they were too shy to emerge from the water to receive their garments. Shri Vitthalnathji returned the Gopis' clothes divinely transformed. That is the Lila of Shri Vitthalnathji."

SHRI DWARKADHEESHJI

Shri Dwarkadheesh, or Dwarkanathji is a four-armed, dark Krishna svarupa. He appeared in ancient times from the Bindu lake and was worshipped by the sage Kapildevaji. During the times of Shri Vallabhacharya, the Blessed Lord appeared to the tailor Narayana in a dream and told him to retrieve His svarupa from a broken shrine at Mount Abu in Rajasthan. Later Shri Vallabhacharya instructed Damodardas Sambhalvare to obtain Shri Dwarkadheesh from the tailor Narayana and begin His seva.

The Lila of Shri Dwarkadheesh arises when He plays hide-and-seek with Shri Radha and the other Gopis. Shri Gusainji explains, "The Shrimad Bhagavatam's five chapters on the Rasa Lila describe how all the Gopis came and sat by the banks of the Yamuna River, surrounding Shri Swaminiji. Shri Thakurji suddenly arrived in the form of Shri Dwarkanathji. With His two lotus hands, Shri Dwarkanathji covered Shri Swaminiji's eyes. He then manifested two additional hands and pleased Her with His flute playing. Shri Dwarkanathji's Lila is filled with nectar."

Shri Dwarkadheesh's lower right hand holds a lotus, which is Radha's palm trying to push Krishna's hand away from Her eyes. His upper right hand holds a mace, and is said to represent Radha's hand moving up to embrace Krishna. The upper left hand holds a discus, representing the impressions left by Radha's bracelets during Their embrace. His lower left hand holds a conch. It reminds Shri Krishna of Radha's neck. Shri Dwarkadheeshji was returned to Shri Vallabhacharya, and when all of the seven svarupas were distributed, Shri Dwarkadheesh was presented to Shri Gusainji's third son, Shri Balkrishnaji.

In 1670 CE, during the times of Aurangzeb, Shri Dwarkadheesh was relocated to Ahmedabad. In 1720 CE He was installed in a palatial mansion in Kankroli, Rajasthan near Nathdvara, where He has remained ever since.

SHRI GOKULNATHJI

Shri Gokulnathji is a small golden Krishna svarupa with two Swaminis, one on each side. His right raised hand holds the Govardhan Hill, while His lower left hand holds a conch. He plays a flute with His other two hands. The Swaminis on either side of Him are Shri Radha and Shri Chandravaliji.

Shri Gokulnathji belonged to the family of Shri Vallabhacharya's wife and was presented to him at the time of their marriage. During Aurangzeb's regime, Shri Gokulnathji moved to Jaipur. In the mid-nineteenth century He returned to Gokul and now resides there, in a Haveli believed to have been constructed around 1511 CE.

Shri Gusainji speaks of His form and Lila: "The form of Shri Gokulnathji appears when Shri Krishna lifted the Govardhan Hill and protected all the Vraja bhaktas. He picked up the Hill with His left hand and then held it with His right hand while playing the flute with His other two hands, filling all the residents of Vraja with nectar. Sometimes He even held the Hill with the end of His flute. Shri Gokulnathji's lower left hand holds the conch, the divine form of water."

SHRI GOKULCHANDRAMAJI

Shri Gokul Chandramaji is the Moon of Gokul and stands in a *tribhangi* posture, bent in three places, His legs crossed at the ankles. He is poised to play the flute. A Kshatriya woman found Him and Shri Navanita Priyaji in the Yamuna River while she was on her way to Mahavan. She presented the svarupas to Shri Vallabhacharya, who then established Shri Gokulchandramaji in the home of his follower, Narayanadas Brahamachari. After Narayanadas passed away, Shri Gokul Chandramaji returned to Shri Vallabhacharya's family, and Shri Gusainji later entrusted Him to his fifth son, Raghunathji.

During Aurangzeb's reign, Shri Gokulchandramaji was taken to Jaipur and then in 1687 CE to Bikaner, Rajasthan, where the ruler, Sardar Singh, was a great devotee of the Pushti Marg. Shri Gokulchandramaji resided there for six years before shifting to Kamvan in Vraja, where He resides today. Shri Gusainji speaks of this divine form of Shri Krishna, "Shri Gokulchandramaji entices even the love god, the enchanter of all other hearts. When Shri Krishna disappeared from the Gopis, they cried for their Beloved. Then Shri Krishna appeared before them as Shri Gokulchandramaji, with a lovely form bent in three places.

He danced the Rasa Lila with the Gopis, played the flute, and gave all the bhaktas of Vrindavan the gift of His own nectar. The seven holes in the Blessed Lord's flute are His six divine virtues plus His Dharmi aspect, wherein He contains the other six virtues. Krishna places His fingers over those holes and consoles the bhaktas, 'I am under the control of your loving devotion. I will always be in debt to you.' Shri Gokulchandramaji also makes Rasa Lila, and His appearance is full of divine elements."

SHRI BALKRISHNAJI, SHRI KALYANRAYAJI, AND SHRI MUKUNDARAYAJI

The small Shri Balkrishnaji svarupa, who was among the Nidhi svarupas present in Shri Gusainji's 7-Nidhi svarupa manorath, was presented by Shri Gusainji to his sixth son, Yadunathji. However, Yadunathji preferred to worship the svarupa of Shri Dwarkadheeshji together with his elder brother (Shri Gusainji's third son, also named Shri Balkrishnaji). He therefore placed the Child Krishna svarupa of Balkrishnaji just in front of Shri Dwarkadheeshji. Balkrishnaji was later taken from Kankroli to Surat, where He resides today.

The dark, four armed Krishna form of Shri Kalyanrayaji, now residing in Baroda, is worshipped by Shri Yadunathji's direct descendants. Shri Yadunathji's sons were granted this seva by Shri Gokulnathji (Shri Gusainji's fourth son). Shri Gusainji's seven sons all learned to make Shri Krishna's adornment with Shri Kalyanrayaji.

Shri Mukundarayaji, a form of infant Krishna, was originally worshipped by Sanchora Ramdas, a *Mukhiya* (head assistant) in Shri Nathji's temple. Ramdas entrusted Shri Mukundarayaji to the bhakta Padmanabhdas, who worshipped Mukundarayaji together with his own svarupa,

Lila	The loving plays and pastimes of Shri Krishna
Mandir	The temple housed within a Pushtimarg Haveli, or home-temple complex
Mangala	Literally, 'auspicious,' this term also refers to the morning and Krishna's morning darshan
Manorath	Literally, the 'chariot which carries the mind-heart,' this refers to a special heart's desire one feels to make an offering or celebration for one's Lord
Pakhavaj	The classical two-headed wooden drum which is used in the Pushti Marg temple singing (Haveli Dhrupad kirtan)
Prasad/Mahaprasad	Food which has been offered to and enjoyed by the Lord becomes prasad, which literally means 'grace.'
Pushti	Grace, and nourishment which arises through that grace
Pushti Marg	The Path of Grace, established by Shri Vallabhacharya and maintained by his descendants
Rajbhog	The main noon-time meal offered to Krishna and the darshan which opens just after Krishna has enjoyed lunch
Rasa Lila	The circular dance and associated Lilas which Krishna plays with the Gopis in the forest
Sakha	Intimate male friend (Gopa)

Sakhi	Intimate female friend (Gopi)
Sandhya	The late afternoon darshan when Krishna is welcomed home from grazing His cows in the forest
Sandhya Prayers	Ritual prayers performed daily by Brahmins
Satsang	True association; devotional company with practitioners and teachers
Seva	The loving service of Krishna, the main practice of the Path of Grace
Sevak	One who performs Krishna's divine service, in the temple or in their own home; a disciple or follower of a particular guru
Shayan	The evening darshan just before Shri Krishna is put to rest for the night
Shri	Divine Beauty; the Goddess; a respectful title preceding sacred beings, teachers, and even towns (i.e. Shri Krishna, Shri Vallabhacharya, Shri Nathdvara)
Shri Acharyaji	Shri Mahaprabhu Vallabhacharya
Shri Gokulnathji	(1551-1640 or -1647) Fourth son of Shri Gusainji; author of the *252 Vaishnavas, 84 Vaishnavas* and many other important texts in Sanskrit and Vrajbhasha
Shri Gusainji	(1516-1586) Second son of Shri Vallabhacharya. He is also known by his birth name, Shri Vitthalnathji.

Shri Harirayaji:	(1590-1715) Grandson of Shri Vitthalnathji's second son and commentator on the 252 *Vaishnavas, 84 Vaishnavas* as well as author of "Shiksha Patra" and other texts. He is credited with great devotional powers and, like Shri Vallabhacharya, is also honored with the title "Mahaprabhu"
Shri Vallabhacharya	(1478-1530) The fourth and last of the great Vaishnava Acharyas. Born to a Tailanga family in the forest at Champaranya, he established the Path of Grace and is the incarnation of Shri Krishna's face.
Shrimad Bhagavatam	The Bhagavat Purana, the text which details the Lilas of Shri Krishna
Shringar	Ornamentation of Krishna with jewels and cloth, and the darshan period which opens in the temple after Krishna has been dressed
Shri Subodhini	Shri Mahaprabhu Vallabhacharya's commentary on the Shrimad Bhagavatam
Svarupa	Literally, 'True Form,' a svarupa is a physical form of the Lord, such as the forms of Shri Krishna worshipped in the Path of Grace
Thakurji	The Lord, Shri Krishna
Tilak	A forehead adornment, which for Pushti Marg Vaishnavas is a red U shape

Utsav	A festival celebration
Utthapan	The period of time and darshan during which Krishna awakes in the forest after taking rest
Vaishnava	A follower of Vishnu; a follower of Krishna and the Path of Grace
Vallabhkul	The lineage of direct descendants of Shri Vallabhacharya
Varta	An account or story, such as the life-accounts of Shri Gusainji's 252 and Shri Mahaprabhuji's 84 Vaishnava disciples
Vedanta	Literally, the 'end of wisdom,' these are the scriptures and philosophies which describe the nature of and path to Supreme Reality
Vraj	The land of Shri Krishna's appearance and lilas, and where Shri Nathji resided at the time of the Ashta Chhap poets. Vaishnavas often perform the 252 kilometer circumambulation of Vraj. Pilgrims walk around Vraj visiting the *baithaks* of Shri Vallabhacharya and Shri Gusainji, as well as the twelve forests and the lakes, all of which are associated with the lilas of Shri Krishna.
Vrajbhasha	The language of Vraj; Shri Krishna's own native language
Vrajvasi	A resident of the area of Vraj